CHMM

Exam Secrets Study Guide

DEAR FUTURE EXAM SUCCESS STORY

First of all, **THANK YOU** for purchasing Mometrix study materials!

Second, congratulations! You are one of the few determined test-takers who are committed to doing whatever it takes to excel on your exam. **You have come to the right place.** We developed these study materials with one goal in mind: to deliver you the information you need in a format that's concise and easy to use.

In addition to optimizing your guide for the content of the test, we've outlined our recommended steps for breaking down the preparation process into small, attainable goals so you can make sure you stay on track.

We've also analyzed the entire test-taking process, identifying the most common pitfalls and showing how you can overcome them and be ready for any curveball the test throws you.

Standardized testing is one of the biggest obstacles on your road to success, which only increases the importance of doing well in the high-pressure, high-stakes environment of test day. Your results on this test could have a significant impact on your future, and this guide provides the information and practical advice to help you achieve your full potential on test day.

Your success is our success

We would love to hear from you! If you would like to share the story of your exam success or if you have any questions or comments in regard to our products, please contact us at **800-673-8175** or **support@mometrix.com**.

Thanks again for your business and we wish you continued success!

Sincerely,
The Mometrix Test Preparation Team

Need more help? Check out our flashcards at:
http://mometrixflashcards.com/CHMM

Written and edited by the Mometrix Exam Secrets Test Prep Team
Printed in the United States of America

TABLE OF CONTENTS

Introduction

Thank you for purchasing this resource! You have made the choice to prepare yourself for a test that could have a huge impact on your future, and this guide is designed to help you be fully ready for test day. Obviously, it's important to have a solid understanding of the test material, but you also need to be prepared for the unique environment and stressors of the test, so that you can perform to the best of your abilities.

For this purpose, the first section that appears in this guide is the **Secret Keys**. We've devoted countless hours to meticulously researching what works and what doesn't, and we've boiled down our findings to the five most impactful steps you can take to improve your performance on the test. We start at the beginning with study planning and move through the preparation process, all the way to the testing strategies that will help you get the most out of what you know when you're finally sitting in front of the test.

We recommend that you start preparing for your test as far in advance as possible. However, if you've bought this guide as a last-minute study resource and only have a few days before your test, we recommend that you skip over the first two Secret Keys since they address a long-term study plan.

If you struggle with **test anxiety**, we strongly encourage you to check out our recommendations for how you can overcome it. Test anxiety is a formidable foe, but it can be beaten, and we want to make sure you have the tools you need to defeat it.

Secret Key #1 – Plan Big, Study Small

There's a lot riding on your performance. If you want to ace this test, you're going to need to keep your skills sharp and the material fresh in your mind. You need a plan that lets you review everything you need to know while still fitting in your schedule. We'll break this strategy down into three categories.

Information Organization

Start with the information you already have: the official test outline. From this, you can make a complete list of all the concepts you need to cover before the test. Organize these concepts into groups that can be studied together, and create a list of any related vocabulary you need to learn so you can brush up on any difficult terms. You'll want to keep this vocabulary list handy once you actually start studying since you may need to add to it along the way.

Time Management

Once you have your set of study concepts, decide how to spread them out over the time you have left before the test. Break your study plan into small, clear goals so you have a manageable task for each day and know exactly what you're doing. Then just focus on one small step at a time. When you manage your time this way, you don't need to spend hours at a time studying. Studying a small block of content for a short period each day helps you retain information better and avoid stressing over how much you have left to do. You can relax knowing that you have a plan to cover everything in time. In order for this strategy to be effective though, you have to start studying early and stick to your schedule. Avoid the exhaustion and futility that comes from last-minute cramming!

Study Environment

The environment you study in has a big impact on your learning. Studying in a coffee shop, while probably more enjoyable, is not likely to be as fruitful as studying in a quiet room. It's important to keep distractions to a minimum. You're only planning to study for a short block of time, so make the most of it. Don't pause to check your phone or get up to find a snack. It's also important to **avoid multitasking**. Research has consistently shown that multitasking will make your studying dramatically less effective. Your study area should also be comfortable and well-lit so you don't have the distraction of straining your eyes or sitting on an uncomfortable chair.

The time of day you study is also important. You want to be rested and alert. Don't wait until just before bedtime. Study when you'll be most likely to comprehend and remember. Even better, if you know what time of day your test will be, set that time aside for study. That way your brain will be used to working on that subject at that specific time and you'll have a better chance of recalling information.

Finally, it can be helpful to team up with others who are studying for the same test. Your actual studying should be done in as isolated an environment as possible, but the work of organizing the information and setting up the study plan can be divided up. In between study sessions, you can discuss with your teammates the concepts that you're all studying and quiz each other on the details. Just be sure that your teammates are as serious about the test as you are. If you find that your study time is being replaced with social time, you might need to find a new team.

Secret Key #2 – Make Your Studying Count

You're devoting a lot of time and effort to preparing for this test, so you want to be absolutely certain it will pay off. This means doing more than just reading the content and hoping you can remember it on test day. It's important to make every minute of study count. There are two main areas you can focus on to make your studying count.

Retention

It doesn't matter how much time you study if you can't remember the material. You need to make sure you are retaining the concepts. To check your retention of the information you're learning, try recalling it at later times with minimal prompting. Try carrying around flashcards and glance at one or two from time to time or ask a friend who's also studying for the test to quiz you.

To enhance your retention, look for ways to put the information into practice so that you can apply it rather than simply recalling it. If you're using the information in practical ways, it will be much easier to remember. Similarly, it helps to solidify a concept in your mind if you're not only reading it to yourself but also explaining it to someone else. Ask a friend to let you teach them about a concept you're a little shaky on (or speak aloud to an imaginary audience if necessary). As you try to summarize, define, give examples, and answer your friend's questions, you'll understand the concepts better and they will stay with you longer. Finally, step back for a big picture view and ask yourself how each piece of information fits with the whole subject. When you link the different concepts together and see them working together as a whole, it's easier to remember the individual components.

Finally, practice showing your work on any multi-step problems, even if you're just studying. Writing out each step you take to solve a problem will help solidify the process in your mind, and you'll be more likely to remember it during the test.

Modality

Modality simply refers to the means or method by which you study. Choosing a study modality that fits your own individual learning style is crucial. No two people learn best in exactly the same way, so it's important to know your strengths and use them to your advantage.

For example, if you learn best by visualization, focus on visualizing a concept in your mind and draw an image or a diagram. Try color-coding your notes, illustrating them, or creating symbols that will trigger your mind to recall a learned concept. If you learn best by hearing or discussing information, find a study partner who learns the same way or read aloud to yourself. Think about how to put the information in your own words. Imagine that you are giving a lecture on the topic and record yourself so you can listen to it later.

For any learning style, flashcards can be helpful. Organize the information so you can take advantage of spare moments to review. Underline key words or phrases. Use different colors for different categories. Mnemonic devices (such as creating a short list in which every item starts with the same letter) can also help with retention. Find what works best for you and use it to store the information in your mind most effectively and easily.

Secret Key #3 – Practice the Right Way

Your success on test day depends not only on how many hours you put into preparing, but also on whether you prepared the right way. It's good to check along the way to see if your studying is paying off. One of the most effective ways to do this is by taking practice tests to evaluate your progress. Practice tests are useful because they show exactly where you need to improve. Every time you take a practice test, pay special attention to these three groups of questions:

- The questions you got wrong
- The questions you had to guess on, even if you guessed right
- The questions you found difficult or slow to work through

This will show you exactly what your weak areas are, and where you need to devote more study time. Ask yourself why each of these questions gave you trouble. Was it because you didn't understand the material? Was it because you didn't remember the vocabulary? Do you need more repetitions on this type of question to build speed and confidence? Dig into those questions and figure out how you can strengthen your weak areas as you go back to review the material.

Additionally, many practice tests have a section explaining the answer choices. It can be tempting to read the explanation and think that you now have a good understanding of the concept. However, an explanation likely only covers part of the question's broader context. Even if the explanation makes perfect sense, **go back and investigate** every concept related to the question until you're positive you have a thorough understanding.

As you go along, keep in mind that the practice test is just that: practice. Memorizing these questions and answers will not be very helpful on the actual test because it is unlikely to have any of the same exact questions. If you only know the right answers to the sample questions, you won't be prepared for the real thing. **Study the concepts** until you understand them fully, and then you'll be able to answer any question that shows up on the test.

It's important to wait on the practice tests until you're ready. If you take a test on your first day of study, you may be overwhelmed by the amount of material covered and how much you need to learn. Work up to it gradually.

On test day, you'll need to be prepared for answering questions, managing your time, and using the test-taking strategies you've learned. It's a lot to balance, like a mental marathon that will have a big impact on your future. Like training for a marathon, you'll need to start slowly and work your way up. When test day arrives, you'll be ready.

Start with the strategies you've read in the first two Secret Keys—plan your course and study in the way that works best for you. If you have time, consider using multiple study resources to get different approaches to the same concepts. It can be helpful to see difficult concepts from more than one angle. Then find a good source for practice tests. Many times, the test website will suggest potential study resources or provide sample tests.

Practice Test Strategy

If you're able to find at least three practice tests, we recommend this strategy:

Untimed and Open-Book Practice

Take the first test with no time constraints and with your notes and study guide handy. Take your time and focus on applying the strategies you've learned.

Timed and Open-Book Practice

Take the second practice test open-book as well, but set a timer and practice pacing yourself to finish in time.

Timed and Closed-Book Practice

Take any other practice tests as if it were test day. Set a timer and put away your study materials. Sit at a table or desk in a quiet room, imagine yourself at the testing center, and answer questions as quickly and accurately as possible.

Keep repeating timed and closed-book tests on a regular basis until you run out of practice tests or it's time for the actual test. Your mind will be ready for the schedule and stress of test day, and you'll be able to focus on recalling the material you've learned.

Secret Key #4 – Pace Yourself

Once you're fully prepared for the material on the test, your biggest challenge on test day will be managing your time. Just knowing that the clock is ticking can make you panic even if you have plenty of time left. Work on pacing yourself so you can build confidence against the time constraints of the exam. Pacing is a difficult skill to master, especially in a high-pressure environment, so **practice is vital**.

Set time expectations for your pace based on how much time is available. For example, if a section has 60 questions and the time limit is 30 minutes, you know you have to average 30 seconds or less per question in order to answer them all. Although 30 seconds is the hard limit, set 25 seconds per question as your goal, so you reserve extra time to spend on harder questions. When you budget extra time for the harder questions, you no longer have any reason to stress when those questions take longer to answer.

Don't let this time expectation distract you from working through the test at a calm, steady pace, but keep it in mind so you don't spend too much time on any one question. Recognize that taking extra time on one question you don't understand may keep you from answering two that you do understand later in the test. If your time limit for a question is up and you're still not sure of the answer, mark it and move on, and come back to it later if the time and the test format allow. If the testing format doesn't allow you to return to earlier questions, just make an educated guess; then put it out of your mind and move on.

On the easier questions, be careful not to rush. It may seem wise to hurry through them so you have more time for the challenging ones, but it's not worth missing one if you know the concept and just didn't take the time to read the question fully. Work efficiently but make sure you understand the question and have looked at all of the answer choices, since more than one may seem right at first.

Even if you're paying attention to the time, you may find yourself a little behind at some point. You should speed up to get back on track, but do so wisely. Don't panic; just take a few seconds less on each question until you're caught up. Don't guess without thinking, but do look through the answer choices and eliminate any you know are wrong. If you can get down to two choices, it is often worthwhile to guess from those. Once you've chosen an answer, move on and don't dwell on any that you skipped or had to hurry through. If a question was taking too long, chances are it was one of the harder ones, so you weren't as likely to get it right anyway.

On the other hand, if you find yourself getting ahead of schedule, it may be beneficial to slow down a little. The more quickly you work, the more likely you are to make a careless mistake that will affect your score. You've budgeted time for each question, so don't be afraid to spend that time. Practice an efficient but careful pace to get the most out of the time you have.

Secret Key #5 – Have a Plan for Guessing

When you're taking the test, you may find yourself stuck on a question. Some of the answer choices seem better than others, but you don't see the one answer choice that is obviously correct. What do you do?

The scenario described above is very common, yet most test takers have not effectively prepared for it. Developing and practicing a plan for guessing may be one of the single most effective uses of your time as you get ready for the exam.

In developing your plan for guessing, there are three questions to address:

- When should you start the guessing process?
- How should you narrow down the choices?
- Which answer should you choose?

When to Start the Guessing Process

Unless your plan for guessing is to select C every time (which, despite its merits, is not what we recommend), you need to leave yourself enough time to apply your answer elimination strategies. Since you have a limited amount of time for each question, that means that if you're going to give yourself the best shot at guessing correctly, you have to decide quickly whether or not you will guess.

Of course, the best-case scenario is that you don't have to guess at all, so first, see if you can answer the question based on your knowledge of the subject and basic reasoning skills. Focus on the key words in the question and try to jog your memory of related topics. Give yourself a chance to bring the knowledge to mind, but once you realize that you don't have (or you can't access) the knowledge you need to answer the question, it's time to start the guessing process.

It's almost always better to start the guessing process too early than too late. It only takes a few seconds to remember something and answer the question from knowledge. Carefully eliminating wrong answer choices takes longer. Plus, going through the process of eliminating answer choices can actually help jog your memory.

Summary: Start the guessing process as soon as you decide that you can't answer the question based on your knowledge.

How to Narrow Down the Choices

The next chapter in this book (**Test-Taking Strategies**) includes a wide range of strategies for how to approach questions and how to look for answer choices to eliminate. You will definitely want to read those carefully, practice them, and figure out which ones work best for you. Here though, we're going to address a mindset rather than a particular strategy.

Your odds of guessing an answer correctly depend on how many options you are choosing from.

Number of options left	5	4	3	2	1
Odds of guessing correctly	20%	25%	33%	50%	100%

You can see from this chart just how valuable it is to be able to eliminate incorrect answers and make an educated guess, but there are two things that many test takers do that cause them to miss out on the benefits of guessing:

- Accidentally eliminating the correct answer
- Selecting an answer based on an impression

We'll look at the first one here, and the second one in the next section.

To avoid accidentally eliminating the correct answer, we recommend a thought exercise called **the $5 challenge**. In this challenge, you only eliminate an answer choice from contention if you are willing to bet $5 on it being wrong. Why $5? Five dollars is a small but not insignificant amount of money. It's an amount you could afford to lose but wouldn't want to throw away. And while losing $5 once might not hurt too much, doing it twenty times will set you back $100. In the same way, each small decision you make—eliminating a choice here, guessing on a question there—won't by itself impact your score very much, but when you put them all together, they can make a big difference. By holding each answer choice elimination decision to a higher standard, you can reduce the risk of accidentally eliminating the correct answer.

The $5 challenge can also be applied in a positive sense: If you are willing to bet $5 that an answer choice *is* correct, go ahead and mark it as correct.

Summary: Only eliminate an answer choice if you are willing to bet $5 that it is wrong.

Which Answer to Choose

You're taking the test. You've run into a hard question and decided you'll have to guess. You've eliminated all the answer choices you're willing to bet $5 on. Now you have to pick an answer. Why do we even need to talk about this? Why can't you just pick whichever one you feel like when the time comes?

The answer to these questions is that if you don't come into the test with a plan, you'll rely on your impression to select an answer choice, and if you do that, you risk falling into a trap. The test writers know that everyone who takes their test will be guessing on some of the questions, so they intentionally write wrong answer choices to seem plausible. You still have to pick an answer though, and if the wrong answer choices are designed to look right, how can you ever be sure that you're not falling for their trap? The best solution we've found to this dilemma is to take the decision out of your hands entirely. Here is the process we recommend:

Once you've eliminated any choices that you are confident (willing to bet $5) are wrong, select the first remaining choice as your answer.

Whether you choose to select the first remaining choice, the second, or the last, the important thing is that you use some preselected standard. Using this approach guarantees that you will not be enticed into selecting an answer choice that looks right, because you are not basing your decision on how the answer choices look.

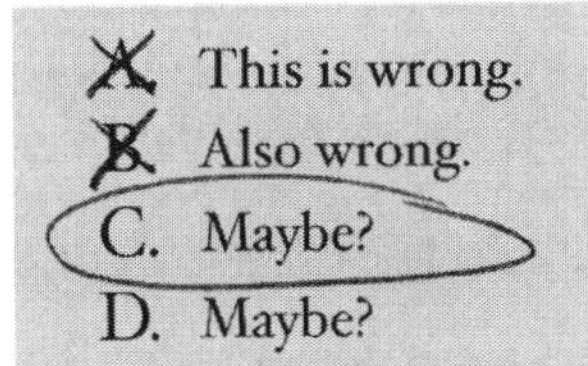

This is not meant to make you question your knowledge. Instead, it is to help you recognize the difference between your knowledge and your impressions. There's a huge difference between thinking an answer is right because of what you know, and thinking an answer is right because it looks or sounds like it should be right.

Summary: To ensure that your selection is appropriately random, make a predetermined selection from among all answer choices you have not eliminated.

Test-Taking Strategies

This section contains a list of test-taking strategies that you may find helpful as you work through the test. By taking what you know and applying logical thought, you can maximize your chances of answering any question correctly!

It is very important to realize that every question is different and every person is different: no single strategy will work on every question, and no single strategy will work for every person. That's why we've included all of them here, so you can try them out and determine which ones work best for different types of questions and which ones work best for you.

Question Strategies

⊘ Read Carefully

Read the question and the answer choices carefully. Don't miss the question because you misread the terms. You have plenty of time to read each question thoroughly and make sure you understand what is being asked. Yet a happy medium must be attained, so don't waste too much time. You must read carefully and efficiently.

⊘ Contextual Clues

Look for contextual clues. If the question includes a word you are not familiar with, look at the immediate context for some indication of what the word might mean. Contextual clues can often give you all the information you need to decipher the meaning of an unfamiliar word. Even if you can't determine the meaning, you may be able to narrow down the possibilities enough to make a solid guess at the answer to the question.

⊘ Prefixes

If you're having trouble with a word in the question or answer choices, try dissecting it. Take advantage of every clue that the word might include. Prefixes can be a huge help. Usually, they allow you to determine a basic meaning. *Pre-* means before, *post-* means after, *pro-* is positive, *de-* is negative. From prefixes, you can get an idea of the general meaning of the word and try to put it into context.

⊘ Hedge Words

Watch out for critical hedge words, such as *likely, may, can, sometimes, often, almost, mostly, usually, generally, rarely,* and *sometimes.* Question writers insert these hedge phrases to cover every possibility. Often an answer choice will be wrong simply because it leaves no room for exception. Be on guard for answer choices that have definitive words such as *exactly* and *always.*

⊘ Switchback Words

Stay alert for *switchbacks.* These are the words and phrases frequently used to alert you to shifts in thought. The most common switchback words are *but, although,* and *however.* Others include *nevertheless, on the other hand, even though, while, in spite of, despite,* and *regardless of.* Switchback words are important to catch because they can change the direction of the question or an answer choice.

✓ Face Value

When in doubt, use common sense. Accept the situation in the problem at face value. Don't read too much into it. These problems will not require you to make wild assumptions. If you have to go beyond creativity and warp time or space in order to have an answer choice fit the question, then you should move on and consider the other answer choices. These are normal problems rooted in reality. The applicable relationship or explanation may not be readily apparent, but it is there for you to figure out. Use your common sense to interpret anything that isn't clear.

Answer Choice Strategies

✓ Answer Selection

The most thorough way to pick an answer choice is to identify and eliminate wrong answers until only one is left, then confirm it is the correct answer. Sometimes an answer choice may immediately seem right, but be careful. The test writers will usually put more than one reasonable answer choice on each question, so take a second to read all of them and make sure that the other choices are not equally obvious. As long as you have time left, it is better to read every answer choice than to pick the first one that looks right without checking the others.

✓ Answer Choice Families

An answer choice family consists of two (in rare cases, three) answer choices that are very similar in construction and cannot all be true at the same time. If you see two answer choices that are direct opposites or parallels, one of them is usually the correct answer. For instance, if one answer choice says that quantity *x* increases and another either says that quantity *x* decreases (opposite) or says that quantity *y* increases (parallel), then those answer choices would fall into the same family. An answer choice that doesn't match the construction of the answer choice family is more likely to be incorrect. Most questions will not have answer choice families, but when they do appear, you should be prepared to recognize them.

✓ Eliminate Answers

Eliminate answer choices as soon as you realize they are wrong, but make sure you consider all possibilities. If you are eliminating answer choices and realize that the last one you are left with is also wrong, don't panic. Start over and consider each choice again. There may be something you missed the first time that you will realize on the second pass.

✓ Avoid Fact Traps

Don't be distracted by an answer choice that is factually true but doesn't answer the question. You are looking for the choice that answers the question. Stay focused on what the question is asking for so you don't accidentally pick an answer that is true but incorrect. Always go back to the question and make sure the answer choice you've selected actually answers the question and is not merely a true statement.

✓ Extreme Statements

In general, you should avoid answers that put forth extreme actions as standard practice or proclaim controversial ideas as established fact. An answer choice that states the "process should be used in certain situations, if..." is much more likely to be correct than one that states the "process should be discontinued completely." The first is a calm rational statement and doesn't even make a definitive, uncompromising stance, using a hedge word *if* to provide wiggle room, whereas the second choice is far more extreme.

☑ Benchmark

As you read through the answer choices and you come across one that seems to answer the question well, mentally select that answer choice. This is not your final answer, but it's the one that will help you evaluate the other answer choices. The one that you selected is your benchmark or standard for judging each of the other answer choices. Every other answer choice must be compared to your benchmark. That choice is correct until proven otherwise by another answer choice beating it. If you find a better answer, then that one becomes your new benchmark. Once you've decided that no other choice answers the question as well as your benchmark, you have your final answer.

☑ Predict the Answer

Before you even start looking at the answer choices, it is often best to try to predict the answer. When you come up with the answer on your own, it is easier to avoid distractions and traps because you will know exactly what to look for. The right answer choice is unlikely to be word-for-word what you came up with, but it should be a close match. Even if you are confident that you have the right answer, you should still take the time to read each option before moving on.

General Strategies

☑ Tough Questions

If you are stumped on a problem or it appears too hard or too difficult, don't waste time. Move on! Remember though, if you can quickly check for obviously incorrect answer choices, your chances of guessing correctly are greatly improved. Before you completely give up, at least try to knock out a couple of possible answers. Eliminate what you can and then guess at the remaining answer choices before moving on.

☑ Check Your Work

Since you will probably not know every term listed and the answer to every question, it is important that you get credit for the ones that you do know. Don't miss any questions through careless mistakes. If at all possible, try to take a second to look back over your answer selection and make sure you've selected the correct answer choice and haven't made a costly careless mistake (such as marking an answer choice that you didn't mean to mark). This quick double check should more than pay for itself in caught mistakes for the time it costs.

☑ Pace Yourself

It's easy to be overwhelmed when you're looking at a page full of questions; your mind is confused and full of random thoughts, and the clock is ticking down faster than you would like. Calm down and maintain the pace that you have set for yourself. Especially as you get down to the last few minutes of the test, don't let the small numbers on the clock make you panic. As long as you are on track by monitoring your pace, you are guaranteed to have time for each question.

☑ Don't Rush

It is very easy to make errors when you are in a hurry. Maintaining a fast pace in answering questions is pointless if it makes you miss questions that you would have gotten right otherwise. Test writers like to include distracting information and wrong answers that seem right. Taking a little extra time to avoid careless mistakes can make all the difference in your test score. Find a pace that allows you to be confident in the answers that you select.

⊘ KEEP MOVING

Panicking will not help you pass the test, so do your best to stay calm and keep moving. Taking deep breaths and going through the answer elimination steps you practiced can help to break through a stress barrier and keep your pace.

Final Notes

The combination of a solid foundation of content knowledge and the confidence that comes from practicing your plan for applying that knowledge is the key to maximizing your performance on test day. As your foundation of content knowledge is built up and strengthened, you'll find that the strategies included in this chapter become more and more effective in helping you quickly sift through the distractions and traps of the test to isolate the correct answer.

Now that you're preparing to move forward into the test content chapters of this book, be sure to keep your goal in mind. As you read, think about how you will be able to apply this information on the test. If you've already seen sample questions for the test and you have an idea of the question format and style, try to come up with questions of your own that you can answer based on what you're reading. This will give you valuable practice applying your knowledge in the same ways you can expect to on test day.

Good luck and good studying!

Planning for Materials with Hazards

Hazardous Material Classes

Hazardous Material

A **hazardous material** is generally considered to be any substance that can cause harm to people or the environment. These are substances that present **health hazards** or **physical hazards** or that can impact the environment. Several agencies have promulgated slightly different definitions of hazardous materials, which may be referred with terms such as "hazardous chemicals" or "dangerous goods."

The Department of Transportation (DOT) defines a hazardous material as "any substance or material...capable of posing an unreasonable risk to safety, health, and property..." (49 CFR 171.8)

The International Air Transportation Association (IATA) uses the term "dangerous goods" to refer to materials that are "...articles or substances which are capable of posing a risk to health, safety, property, or the environment..." as listed in the Dangerous Goods Regulation (DGR).

The Occupational Safety and Health Administration (OSHA) defines a **hazardous chemical** as any chemical that presents a physical or health hazard, including combustible dusts and simple asphyxiants (29 CFR 1910.1200).

Chemical Hazard Classes

The **Globally Harmonized System** of Classification and Labelling of Chemicals **(GHS)** uses a system of **hazard classes** for all chemicals in communicating chemical hazards. A chemical may belong to more than one class based on its properties. Those classes are:

- Physical Hazards
  - Explosives
  - Flammable Gases
  - Flammable Aerosols
  - Oxidizing Gases
  - Gases Under Pressure
  - Flammable Liquids
  - Flammable Solids
  - Self-Reactive Substances
  - Pyrophoric Liquids
  - Pyrophoric Solids
  - Self-Heating Substances
  - Substances Which in Contact with Water Emit Flammable Gases
  - Oxidizing Liquids
  - Oxidizing Solids
  - Organic Peroxides
  - Substances Corrosive to Metal
- Health Hazards
  - Acute Toxicity
  - Skin Corrosion
  - Skin Irritation

- Eye Effects
- Sensitization
- Germ Cell Mutagenicity
- Carcinogenicity
- Reproductive Toxicity
- Target Organ Systemic Toxicity: Single Exposure & Repeated Exposure
- Aspiration Toxicity

- Environmental Hazards
    - Acute Aquatic Toxicity
    - Chronic Aquatic Toxicity

Corrosive Materials

According to OSHA

A corrosive substance is one that chemically reacts with a material to cause damage. The Occupational Health and Safety Administration (OSHA) defines a corrosive as a material that causes destruction to the skin or to metal. In the Globally Harmonized System (GHS) of Classification and Labelling of Chemicals, there are three subcategories for corrosives:

1. Skin corrosives/irritants, which are further subdivided into Category 1 (causing full tissue destruction within four hours) and Category 2 (causing redness and pain but not necessarily destroying the dermis)
2. Serious eye irritants, which are further subdivided into Category 1 (causing irreversible eye damage) and Category 2 (causing reversible irritation)
3. Substances corrosive to metals, which decrease the thickness of steel or aluminum at a rate of at least 0.25 inches per year

According to DOT

The Department of Transportation (DOT) classifies corrosives as materials that cause destruction to skin or to metal. The DOT further subdivides the chemicals into **packing groups** based on their **rate of reaction**:

- Packing Group I: chemicals that completely destroy skin in less than three minutes in a 60-minute observation period
- Packing Group II: chemicals that completely destroy skin between three and 60 minutes within a 14-day observation period
- Packing Group III: chemicals that completely destroy skin between one and four hours in a 14-day observation period
- Packing Group IV: chemicals that decrease the thickness of steel or aluminum at a rate of at least 0.25 inches per year.

pH

The term "**pH**" is used in chemistry and describes the **acidity** or **alkalinity** of a water-based solution. It is a logarithmic-scale measure of the concentration of **free protons** in the solution.

The pH scale runs from 0 to 14, where materials with a pH of less than 7 are termed "acids" and those with a pH above 7 are termed "**bases**," "caustics," or "alkaline materials." Solutions with a pH of 7, such as clean water, are termed "**neutral**." The scale is **logarithmic**, meaning that a change of 1 is a tenfold change in the proton concentration. For hazardous materials, the term "corrosive" refers to both acids and bases.

The Environmental Protection Agency (EPA) uses pH to define corrosive hazardous wastes. A waste that has a pH of less than 2 or greater than 12.5 is considered corrosive.

Flash Point

The Occupational Safety and Health Administration (OSHA) defines "**flash point**" as the temperature at which a liquid generates enough vapor to form a flammable mixture with air. At temperatures below the flash point of a given liquid, there are not enough vapors present to provide a **fuel/oxygen ratio** that is adequate for an ignition source to ignite the vapors. Thus, the lower the flash point of a chemical, the more likely it is to present a **flammability hazard** when exposed to a source of ignition.

Flammable and Combustible

The National Fire Prevention Association (NFPA) classifies liquid chemicals that present a flammability hazard into two broad categories based on their flash point: flammable and combustible.

Flammable chemicals are those having flash points at or below 100 degrees F. Flammable chemicals are further subcategorized based on their boiling points as follows:

- **Class IA:** flash point less than 73 F, boiling point less than 100 F
- **Class IB:** flash point less than 73 F, boiling point greater than 100 F
- **Class IC:** flash point greater than 73 F but less than 100 F

Combustible chemicals are those having flash points greater than 100 F. They are also subcategorized, based on their flash points:

- **Class II:** flash point greater than 100 F but less than 140 F
- **Class IIIA:** flash point greater than 140 F but less than 200 F
- **Class IIIB:** flash point greater than 200 F

LD_{50}

The abbreviation "**LD_{50}**" stands for "lethal dose, 50 percent." The LD_{50} is a gauge of the **toxicity** of a material. The LD_{50} value for a given chemical is the amount that, in an animal test, resulted in the death of half (50 percent) of the animal population. "**Dose**" is defined as "the amount of chemical given over a period of time." For the LD_{50}, this refers to the amount of chemical given in a single exposure to a test animal population.

The LD_{50} is expressed in either milligrams per gram (mg/g) or milligrams per kilogram (mg/kg), where the denominator (g or kg) refers to the body weight of the test subject. For example, if a chemical has an LD_{50} of 20 mg/kg, half of the test population did not survive when given 20 mg per 1 kg of the test animal's body weight (a 1 kg animal perished with a 20 mg dose while a 2 kg animal died when given a 40 mg dose).

Thus, a substance that has a low LD_{50} is more toxic than one with a higher LD_{50} because it takes less of the low-LD_{50} substance to cause half of the test population to die.

Health Hazard Categories

The United Nations' Globally Harmonized System (GHS) of Classification and Labelling of Chemicals places chemicals into five categories based on the health hazards they present. The classification is based on published lethal doses (lethal dose, 50 percent values, or LD_{50}, expressed in milligrams per kilogram, or mg/kg) or lethal concentrations (lethal concentration, 50 percent values, or LC_{50}, expressed in parts per million, or ppm) data. Doses and concentrations are also listed based on **exposure route** (oral, dermal, gas, vapor, dust/mist). The lower the LD_{50} or LC_{50}, the more toxic the substance.

Category 1 substances are the most dangerous, having an oral LD_{50} less than 5 mg/kg and a gas LC_{50} less than 100 ppm. **Category 5** substances, the least hazardous of the classifications, have an oral LD_{50} between 2,000 and 5,000 mg/kg (2 – 5 g/kg) and gas LC_{50} above 20,000 ppm.

OSHA's Definition of Health Hazard

The Occupational Safety and Health Administration (OSHA) describes its definition of a health hazard in the Hazard Communication Standard located in 29 CFR 1910.1200. Under this definition, a health hazard is any chemical where the preponderance of evidence demonstrates that the substance causes changes in the biology of humans or test subject animals. This includes **acutely toxic** materials, chemicals that are corrosive to skin, skin irritants or sensitizers, eye damaging chemicals, respiratory sensitizers, **mutagens**, **carcinogens**, **reproductive toxins**, and **specific organ toxins**.

Safety Data Sheets

The Hazard Communication Standard requires that an employer maintain **safety data sheets (SDS)** for any hazardous chemicals that are used or stored on the premises.

An SDS is a sheet prepared by the manufacturer or distributor of the chemical and is used to convey any hazard information to the end user of the product. The SDS is divided into 16 sections, each having different information. The SDS is designed to act as a safety resource for employees who use hazardous chemicals. The SDS contains the name of the chemical and, if the chemical is a mixture, its ingredients. (Some proprietary formulations may be designated as "trade secrets.") The sheet also has the name and contact information of the manufacturer as well as the hazards the material presents. In addition, an SDS specifies safe handling and storage requirements as well as what protective equipment is recommended while using the material. Health effects and exposure limits are presented so that an employee can determine what the safe levels are and what symptoms they could experience if they are exposed to the substance. Other specific information regarding medical treatment and firefighting are also provided on the document, in addition to the chemical and physical properties of the substance.

Identities and Names of Substances or Mixtures

The identity or name of a given material is located in section 1 of the safety data sheet (SDS) for that material. In this section, the manufacturer lists the **product identifier**, which is the name of the substance (either the commercial name or an identifier the manufacturer uses to refer to the substance). In addition to the identifier, a commercial name for the material may be listed, as well as any **synonyms**. For example, on a safety data sheet for sodium hydroxide beads, section 1 may list "caustic soda" and "caustic lye" as other names for the material that the reader may be more familiar with.

Ingredients of Materials

Section 3 of a safety data sheet lists the **composition** and ingredient information of a formulation. In this section, the user can locate the materials present in the formulation. All hazardous ingredients must be listed if they comprise more than 1% of the total or, for carcinogens, if they make up more than 0.1% of the total product. For each ingredient, the list will show the chemical name, the **Chemical Abstracts Service (CAS)** number, and the amount contained in the mixture by percentage. If a compound contains a proprietary component that a manufacturer believes gives them a competitive edge in their market, they can list an ingredient as "trade secret."

Hazard Information

Section 2 is titled "Hazards Identification" and contains information related to the hazards presented by the material and the related warning information. Information in this section includes:

- The **hazard classification** (e.g., corrosive, toxic, flammable)
- Globally Harmonized System (GHS) **signal word** (Warning, Caution)
- GHS hazard statements
- GHS pictograms
- GHS precautionary statements
- Descriptions of hazards not otherwise classified
- If a mixture contains any constituents of **unknown toxicity**, there must be a statement conveying the percentage of the mixture that contains chemicals of unknown toxicity.

Globally Harmonized System of Classification and Labelling of Chemicals Pictograms

The Globally Harmonized System (GHS) of Classification and Labelling of Chemicals incorporates a set of pictograms to quickly convey hazards that a material presents in a way that can be understood regardless of language or reading ability. The format is standardized as a red outline of a square on a point, a white field, and a black symbol. The pictograms are as follows:

- Flame over circle: oxidizer
- Flame: flammable, pyrophoric, self-heating, self-reactive, organic peroxide
- Person with star on chest: carcinogen, mutagen, reproductive toxin, respiratory sensitizer, target organ toxicity, aspiration toxicity
- Exclamation point: skin or eye irritant, skin sensitizer, acutely harmful, narcotic, respiratory irritant
- Gas cylinder: compressed gas
- Test tube with hand and metal plate: corrosion/burns to skin, eye damage, corrosive to metals
- Exploding bomb: explosive, self-reactive, organic peroxide
- Skull and crossbones: acutely toxic (fatal or toxic)
- Tree and dead fish: aquatic toxicity (non-mandatory in the United States)

Hazardous Ingredients of Materials

Whereas all ingredients in a material are listed in section 3, hazardous components are listed in section 8, Exposure Control/Personal Protection. Components of the material that have a published **exposure limit**, including permissible exposure limit (PEL), threshold limit value (TLV), or immediately dangerous to life and health (IDLH), are listed along with the published value. Only materials that present health hazards will be listed in this section.

In addition to the hazardous components, this section will also recommend **engineering controls** to mitigate exposures, recommendations for **personal protective equipment**, and any special considerations for protective equipment.

Physical Properties

Section 9 of a safety data sheet (SDS) lists the physical and chemical properties of the material. Evaluation of this section can assist in identifying both the hazards presented by the material as well as potential **release modes**. There are numerous data points required in section 9, including the following:

- Appearance – describes the material as a liquid, solid, or gas in its native state
- **Vapor pressure** – provides information on the potential of the material presenting an airborne-release hazard
- pH – helps in determining whether a substance is corrosive and whether it as an acid or a base, which is useful for determining the treatments available to mitigate the hazard
- Boiling point – allows inferences about whether the material has airborne-release potential and what conditions cause the material to convert from a liquid to a gas
- Flash point – establishes the classification of a material as a nonflammable, flammable, or combustible material.

Pollution Prevention

Pollution can be defined as the release of harmful substances into the environment. Pollution can have a natural cause, such as a volcanic eruption, or a cause related to human activity, as in the case of air emissions from industrial processes. Air pollutants can be particulates (dusts or vehicle emissions), gases (methane released from petroleum processing), or vapors (evaporation of paint solvents). Water pollutants can include substances that mix with water (sewage discharges), substances that do not mix with water (oil leaks from offshore drilling operations), or solid materials that either mix with water (such as coke ash waste) or do not mix with water (plastic waste). Soil pollutants can be liquid (perchloroethylene from dry-cleaning operations) or solid (lead paint flakes from a house renovation).

Impacts of Pollution on Health and the Environment

Particulate Matter

The impacts of air pollution on health and the environment are well documented by the Environmental Protection Agency (EPA). Particulate matter is classified by the mean average diameter of the particles it contains (for example, **fine particulate matter**, or $\mathbf{PM_{2.5}}$, refers to particulate matter containing particles with an average diameter of 2.5 microns).

Particulate matter having particles with a mean diameter of less than 10 microns ($\mathbf{PM_{10}}$) has known short- and long-term health effects. PM_{10} has been linked to higher occurrences of asthma, heart attacks, and strokes. In addition to health impacts, particulate matter also impacts the environment. Fine particles result in haze that impairs visibility. Other particles may contribute to the acidification of surface water (impacting vegetation) and lead to acid rain.

Gaseous Air Pollutants

Air-polluting gases, including sulfur dioxide, nitrogen oxides, and methane, negatively impact the environment and the health of humans in the area. Ground-level ozone has been linked to asthma attacks and lung damage. Sulfur dioxide has been linked to asthma and respiratory illness as well as acid rain, which damages structures and lowers the pH of ponds and streams. Nitrogen dioxide is also linked to respiratory illnesses and reacts with upper-level ozone to decrease the earth's protection from ultraviolet rays emitted by the sun. Other gases such as methane remain in the atmosphere and trap the convective heat from the earth, which has been proposed to be contributing to a net increase in the earth's temperature.

Water Pollution

Pollutants in the water can have a variety of impacts on people and the environment. In some municipalities, drinking water is pulled from above or below ground waterways. Thus, any pollutants in the source water have the potential to be ingested by people. Organic material discharged in the water will reduce the amount of dissolved oxygen in the water available to aquatic species. Some water pollutants, such as phosphates, can encourage algae growth. Large blooms of algae can impact dissolved oxygen, clog inlets for municipal water systems, and force waterborne animals to relocate. Petroleum products discharged in waterways can reduce aquatic animals' access to oxygen by forming a layer on top of the water, can poison animal food supplies, can negatively impact drinking water, and can directly harm any animal that is exposed to the material.

Soil Pollution

Modes

Soil pollution can be caused by releases, leaks, or improper disposal. Accidents can result in the release or spill of a hazardous material onto the ground. A dropped bag of lime, a rail car accident, or a broken conveyor belt can release materials onto unprotected soil. Underground or aboveground storage tanks can fail over time and leak their contents into the surrounding soil. Unwanted hazardous materials must be managed properly to avoid improper disposal. Abandoned waste containers or containers that are illegally sent to unpermitted facilities can fail over time, releasing waste into the soil.

Impact on Surrounding Communities

The primary risk that soil pollution presents to communities is of hazardous materials **leaching** through the soil into groundwater, where it can then spread quickly. Some communities rely on groundwater as their public water source, and groundwater can become contaminated when a pollutant is released into the soil. Pollutants can migrate horizontally and vertically through the ground (if they are liquids), and they can spread through groundwater. Thus, the material can travel beyond the spill or release area, potentially impacting surrounding communities. Individuals who enter sites that have had chemical releases may be exposed directly to contaminated soil. **Volatile chemicals** can also be released from the soil into the air where they can impact nearby communities.

Pollution Prevention

Pollution Prevention Act

In 1990, Congress passed the **Pollution Prevention Act**. This legislation acknowledged that the United States was annually producing millions of tons of pollution that was requiring billions of dollars to remediate. Thus, Congress acted to encourage businesses to use the concept of **source reduction**, wherein hazardous substances, pollutants, or contaminants are prevented from entering the waste stream during the production process. This includes examining processes for opportunities to reduce hazardous waste by reducing the total amount of hazardous substances used, replacing hazardous substances with nonhazardous or less hazardous alternatives, or utilizing capture technologies to prevent release.

Waste Reduction

The Environmental Protection Agency defines **pollution prevention (P2)** as any practice of reducing, eliminating, or preventing pollution during the production process.

Pollution prevention is the process of evaluating every step of production to reduce waste, from environmentally conscious selection of raw materials to using more recyclable materials considering the end-of-life fate of the product. Pollution prevention also aims to cut down on air pollution by assessing the energy efficiency of equipment. Furthermore, P2 seeks to minimize the use of hazardous chemicals in order to reduce the volume and types of hazardous waste requiring management. Such a program seeks to reduce the overall financial and environmental costs of a production process. The efforts of a P2 program can benefit a corporation by making it leaner, reducing its risk of financial exposure due to pollution, and providing it with a competitive advantage in the "green" economy.

POLLUTION PREVENTION HIERARCHY

Pollution prevention is the concept of eliminating the emission of unwanted materials or waste into soil, air, or water from industrial processes. The Environmental Protection Agency (EPA) has established a recommended five- level hierarchy for pollution prevention programs for businesses.

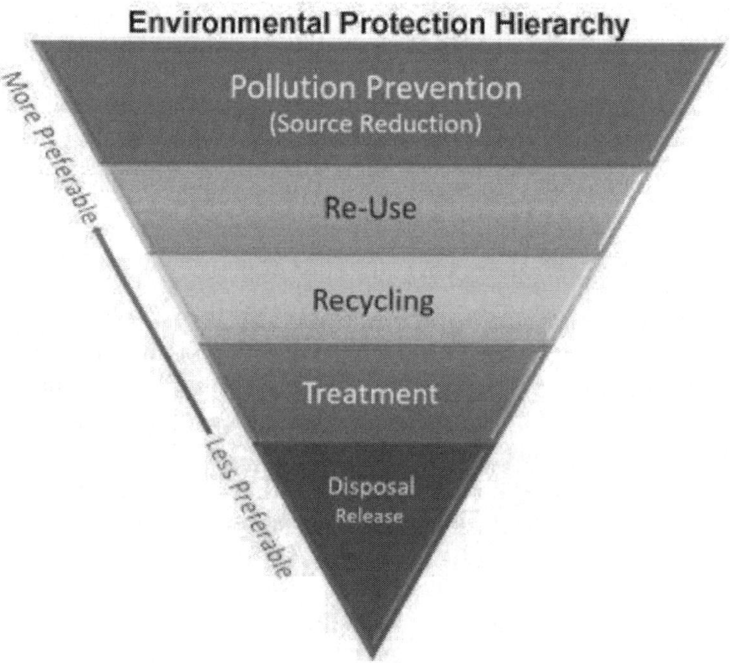

The hierarchy moves from most desirable to least desirable methods, as follows:

- Source reduction – reduction or elimination of the pollutant by reworking the process
- Reuse – capturing pollutants and reinserting them back into the process or another process that requires the same material; typically uses less energy than recycling
- Recycle – capturing pollutants and using them to produce another product
- Treatment – capturing pollutants and rendering them less hazardous or nonhazardous before release or disposal
- Disposal – capturing pollutants and preparing for them for proper permanent storage in a manner that will prevent accidental release during internment

POLLUTION PREVENTION OPPORTUNITY ASSESSMENT

The goal of pollution prevention is to reduce the use of hazardous materials and thereby reduce the risk of pollutant release to as near zero as economically and technically feasible. A **pollution prevention opportunity assessment** (PPOA or P2OA) is a systematic method of evaluating each step in a process to identify opportunities to reduce or eliminate hazardous waste. The reduction of hazardous waste generation reduces costs associated with containment and disposal. Additionally, application of a P2OA can reduce the need for future pollution remediation and reduce the burden of associated environmental compliance.

Outcomes from a P2OA include pollutant source identification, types and amounts of waste generated, and solutions for reducing the generation of pollutants and waste.

Steps

A **pollution prevention opportunity assessment (P2OA)** is a tool for evaluating a process for its environmental impact. The United States Air Force has published a six-step process for conducting a P2OA:

- Step 1 – Identify and select the process. This step entails identifying the process, task, or equipment that will be examined for pollution-reduction potential. Prioritization can be given to processes, tasks, or equipment that generate the most hazardous or highest quantity of waste.
- Step 2 – Select the assessment team. The P2OA team should be a cross-functional group that includes workers, staff, supervisors, maintenance staff, and safety professionals to provide a different perspective on the process.
- Step 3 – Examine the process. All steps of the process are thoroughly examined for opportunities for waste and pollutant reduction, including energy consumption, waste generation, hazardous material utilization, and related costs. Information can be gathered by way of waste records, purchase records, and applicable permits.
- Step 4 – Establish a baseline. A process diagram should be constructed with all materials and wastes listed to provide a baseline consumption or production level.
- Step 5 – Identify opportunities. Through a team effort such as a brainstorming session, opportunities to reduce the amount of hazardous materials consumed or waste generated are identified. Cost considerations should always be included and weighed against potential waste removal and permit cost reductions.
- Step 6 – Rank opportunities. Using a standardized set of criteria, the team should then rank opportunities to provide management with a list for implementation. Rankings should consider cost, worker health and safety improvements, environmental impacts, and feasibility.

Recycling

Recycling is the process of collecting unwanted materials, scrap, waste, or pollutants and using them for new products. Recycling removes materials from waste streams and reduces the amount of waste that must be stored in landfills or storage facilities. From a business perspective, recycling reduces the cost associated with waste management by reducing the total volume that must be managed. For some materials, recyclers may offer free removal or even payment, potentially transforming a cost into a revenue source.

Effective Recycling of Waste Products

The most common example of recycling in the United States is plastic recycling. Containers, packing materials, or scrap may be able to be recycled, thereby reducing a facility's unregulated waste stream costs. Glass is another material that is routinely recycled around the world. Scrap glass that is crushed can be put back into the manufacturing process for new glass (called "cullet"), can be used as a blasting medium, or can be made into fiberglass. Used oil is another example of recycling, wherein the waste oil is processed and repackaged for additional use. Used oil can be repurposed as a mold release in industrial processes, used as burner oil, or further processed to make lubricants.

Clean Air Act

Application of Clean Air Act to Industrial Processes

The **Clean Air Act** of 1970 established **National Ambient Air Quality Standards (NAAQS)** to reduce the public impact of air pollution from industrial sources. NAAQS, which are promulgated by the Environmental Protection Agency (EPA), are established for six contaminants of concern: carbon monoxide, ground-level ozone, lead, nitrogen oxides (NOXs), particulate matter, and sulfur dioxide. NAAQS were coupled with **state implementation plans (SIPs)** to achieve reduction in pollutant levels. The Act is applicable to both stationary (i.e., businesses or factories) and mobile (i.e., diesel-powered equipment) sources. Regional areas that do not meet the established NAAQS are deemed "nonattainment areas." In nonattainment areas, local governments must establish plans to reduce pollutants, which may include imposing additional emission restrictions on businesses.

The act was updated in 1990 with new technological requirements for major sources (those producing 10 tons per year or more of a hazardous air pollutant or 25 tons per year of combined hazardous air pollutants). These emitters are required to install controls, referred to as **maximum achievable control technology (MACT)**, to limit the emission of air pollutants.

Newly constructed stationary sources or those facilities that undergo extensive upgrades or modifications must meet the **new source performance standards (NSPS)** for the listed pollutants. Additionally, each new construction project is subject to a **new source review (NSR)** to determine its potential impact on the local air quality.

Hazardous Air Pollutant

The Environmental Protection Agency (EPA) uses the term "**hazardous air pollutant**" **(HAP)** for any airborne contaminant that is a known or suspected carcinogen or reproductive toxin, that causes birth defects or other serious health effects, or that affects the environment. There are currently 187 listed HAPs, including benzene (from gasoline refining), perchloroethylene (from dry-cleaning businesses), asbestos, and chromium. These substances are also referred to as "air toxics" or "air pollutants." HAPs may be discharged during an industrial process from emissions stacks or vents or due to leaks in a closed system, accidental releases, or material transfer between locations or process stages.

NESHAP

The **National Emission Standards for Hazardous Air Pollutants (NESHAP)** are the Environmental Protection Agency's **stationary source** standards for hazardous air pollutants (HAPs). In Title 40 of the Code of Federal Regulations, NESHAP identifies specific source categories and industries that may emit HAPs. Within the code, NESHAP details application of the standards to facilities, emissions limitations, testing requirements, and compliance requirements.

Thus, every facility must examine the NESHAP source category list to determine if its activities are regulated. If so, the facility must determine what the applicable regulations are, what the emissions standards are, what their emissions are compared to those standards, and how to reduce their emissions of the listed HAPs. Additionally, measures to monitor and report their emissions must be implemented to demonstrate compliance with the standard.

Operating Permit for an Industrial Process

An **operating permit** is a document issued by a state or local agency that allows certain activities to occur. Regarding pollution control, the permit outlines what a facility must do to achieve compliance in reducing pollution emissions. The permit may require the implementation of best available technology (BAT) or maximum achievable control technology (MACT). The document may also delineate the **allowable discharge** limits for specific contaminants. Emissions in excess of the permit must be reported to the local agency, and actions must be taken to prevent future overages.

Permit for Air Emissions

Title V of the Clean Air Act requires that certain businesses obtain an **operating permit** to ensure that their operations do not adversely impact the air quality of the region. Most of these permits are issued and enforced by state agencies. These permits are must be renewed every five years.

A Title V permit is required for businesses for which any of the following is true:

- The business qualifies as a **major source**, meaning they annually emit more than 10 tons of any hazardous air pollutant (HAP), 25 tons of any combination of HAPs, or 100 tons of any air pollutant.
- The business emits more than 50 tons of volatile organic compounds (VOCs) or nitrogen oxides (NOXs).
- The business is subject to the new source performance standards, NESHAPS, or chemical accident provisions.
- The business utilizes on-site solid waste incinerators.
- The business emits more than 100,000 **carbon dioxide-equivalent** tons per year.
- The business is specifically listed in Title V.

Title V Permit

Businesses are required to self-evaluate whether they require a Title V permit for air emissions. Permit applications are obtained from the state agency responsible for monitoring air emissions. State agencies may establish timelines for permit applications, but timelines cannot be shorter than 12 months from the time the operations become subject to the permit program.

Although the exact format of the application may vary by state, all permit applications must include:

- Company name and address
- Facility name and address, if different from the company headquarters
- Description of the business processes and products using **Standard Industrial Classification (SIC)** code
- Emissions information, including all pollutants classified as major and all regulated air pollutants, a description of all point sources of emissions, emission rate expressed in tons per year (tpy), installed pollution control equipment, compliance monitoring equipment or operational controls to reduce emissions,
- Pollution control measures
- Proposed exemptions
- A compliance plan stating that all equipment is in or planned to be in compliance, including how compliance will be achieved and a timeline

Completed permits are submitted to the appropriate agency for review. Reviews also include a **public comment period** after which the permit is either accepted or rejected. If rejected, the business has a 90-day timeframe to revise and resubmit the application. Once the permit is approved, businesses must annually provide compliance monitoring data and renew the permit every five years.

Clean Water Act

Impact of Clean Water Act on Industrial Operations

The Environmental Protection Agency (EPA) is charged, by way of the **Clean Water Act (CWA)**, with regulating the discharge of pollutants into the **waterways** of the United States. The CWA establishes wastewater standards for industry as well as **maximum pollution standards** allowed in surface waters. The CWA makes it illegal to discharge any pollutant into a navigable waterway without a permit.

National Pollutant Discharge Elimination System

The **National Pollutant Discharge Elimination System (NPDES)** is a permit system that regulates point sources of discharge into waterways. A point source is any pipe, drain, or ditch that conveys wastewater into a waterway. Thus, any business that discharges wastewater must have an NPDES permit issued by a local jurisdiction. **Water quality standards** for discharges are established for pH, dissolved solids, particulate matter, certain heavy metals, and organic material (measured by way of biological oxygen demand). Concerns over these contaminants relate not only to their environmental impacts but also to the increased demand placed on municipal treatment plants that may result from the industrial discharge.

Industrial Wastewater

Industrial wastewater is any water that is used in an industrial process that may contain pollutants that can change the chemical or biological properties of the water it is discharged into or that may adversely impact the operations of any publicly owned treatment works (POTW) that treats the wastewater.

Wastewater may be generated in a variety of forms, including coolant water, water used to scrub air emissions, commercial laundry water containing dirt and detergent, chemical manufacturing wastewater, fracking waste, farm water discharges containing pesticides and fertilizers, wastewater from sewage treatment plants, and wastewater from food processing plants.

Point Source in Industrial Wastewater Discharge

Industrial wastewater regulations are applicable to point source discharges into waterways. The Environmental Protection Agency defines a point source as any "discernible, confined, and discrete conveyance." This definition includes pipes, ditches, tunnels, conduits, channels, discrete fissures, or containers. It also pertains to vessels and floating craft that discharge pollutants or may discharge pollutants. A point source can be viewed as any means by which used water is directed into a waterway. The definition does not include agricultural stormwater discharges or irrigation return flows.

Priority Pollutant

A **priority pollutant** is a chemical that is specifically **regulated** by the Environmental Protection Agency (EPA) in wastewater discharges to public waters. The list of chemicals that are considered priority pollutants is located in 40 CFR Part 423 Appendix A. Currently this standard lists 126 pollutants. The EPA has developed and published specific **analytical tests** for the substances that are on the priority pollutant list. The **discharge limits** for those pollutants are listed within the applicable industry guideline documents.

Permit for Industrial Wastewater Discharge

The Clean Water Act (CWA) prohibits the **discharge** of pollutants from a point source into the waters of the United States. The CWA defines **water** as any navigable river, lake, tributary, interstate waters, the ocean out to 200 miles from land, and recreational waters.

If a business discharges wastewater into any such waters, they will need to determine if they require a National Pollution Discharge Elimination System (NPDES) permit. To determine if a particular facility requires a permit, the facility must refer to the list of industries found in Title 40 of the Code of Federal regulations. Title 40 also outlines the **effluent limitations** and **pretreatment requirements** for the wastewater discharged into the waterways. **Pollutant categories** are based on criteria such as **total suspended solids (TSS)**, temperature, pH, biological oxygen demand, chemical oxygen demand, and heavy metals. Treatment standards are "technology based" in that they are based only on the performance of the method and not on the risk to or impact on the receiving waters.

Businesses that discharge wastewater into a sanitary sewer system are not required to obtain an NPDES permit, but local agencies may require separate permitting for this disposal method.

Major and Minor NPDES Permits

A National Pollutant Discharge Elimination System (NPDES) permit specifies the conditions in which a facility may discharge pollutants into a designated waterway and the amount that may be discharged.

Industrial point sources are classified as **major** or **minor** based on a rating sheet that scores several factors of wastewater discharge. Scoring categories, referred to as "**factors**," include:

- Toxic components in effluent
- Volume of effluent
- Oxygen-demand components
- Total suspended solids (TSS)
- Nitrogen-containing pollutants
- Public health **impact** (considers whether there is a public drinking water supply within 50 miles)
- Water quality
- Proximity to coastal water.

The scores are totaled pursuant to the worksheet. If the total score exceeds 80 points, then the permit is deemed to be major. Otherwise, it is considered minor.

Individual and General NPDES Permits

National Pollutant Discharge Elimination System (NPDES) water discharge permits can be issued as individual permits or general permits.

An **individual NPDES permit** is a site-specific permit that is written for a single facility. The permit is unique to the facility and addresses the pollutants being discharged into the water from their specific processes. The individual permit process can take six months or more to receive.

A **general NPDES permit** covers multiple dischargers all of whom have similar operations and pollutant discharge profiles. A general NPDES permit is not written for any specific business as it covers multiple businesses in an area. Advantages of working under a general permit include nearly instantaneous coverage because the permit is already in place and because the business will know its specific pollutant discharge limits before coverage is provided as the permit has already been issued.

Applying for Coverage Under General NPDES Permit

National Pollution Discharge Elimination System (NPDES) **general permits** do not require that a business apply for coverage as the permit is already in place. Instead, the business will submit a **notice of intent (NOI)** to be covered by a pre-existing general permit. The permitting authority, typically a state agency, will receive the NOI from the potential discharger. In general, an NOI will require:

- Name and address of discharge location
- Name and address of parent company, if different from location address
- General permit number under which the business is seeking to be covered
- For each point of discharge, the name of the waterway receiving the discharge, any pre-existing pollutants in the waterway as listed in the Clean Water Act Section 303, and whether a **total maximum daily load (TMDL)** has been completed and what the stated limits are
- Any chemical treatment process to be conducted before wastewater is released into the waterway
- Endangered species declarations
- Evaluation of any sites of historical importance that may be disturbed due to installation of treatment equipment.

Forms are submitted to both the EPA and the state agency.

Applying for Individual NPDES Permit

National Pollution Discharge Elimination System (NPDES) **individual permits** must be applied for at least 180 days prior to any discharge operations. A business applying for a permit must first determine whether they need to submit their application to the Environmental Protection Agency (EPA) or to a state agency.

In general, the permit must include:

- Activities or processes that will result in discharges
- Name and address of the facility
- Up to four Standard Industrial Codes (SIC) or **North American Industry Classification System (NAICS)** codes describing the operations at the facility
- Operator's name and address if different from the facility address
- All permits related to other pollutant classes (e.g., Title V permits, RCRA permits, construction permits, etc.)
- A topographic map of the facility location including a one-mile extension beyond the boundary of the facility
- Description of the nature of the business
- Whether or not the processes use **cooling water** as well as the source of the cooling water
- Any requested **variances**
- If the industry is listed in Appendix A of 40 CFR 122.21, quantitative data for any organic toxic pollutants, toxic metals, cyanide, or total phenols

The permit process includes a public notice requirement. When issued, the permit will list the pollutant limits, monitoring requirements, reporting requirements, and other relevant provisions.

RCRA

The Resource Conservation and Recovery Act (RCRA) permits authorize a facility to treat, store, or dispose of hazardous waste. A site must apply for a permit prior to beginning construction and must renew the permit per periodicity decided by the issuing authority. The permit outlines requirements including the following:

- Facility design and operation
- Required safety standards
- Required monitoring and reporting
- Performance and construction requirements for treatment technologies to be used at the site

State agencies authorized by the Environmental Protection Agency (EPA) issue permits for RCRA waste management facilities. If a state is not authorized, then the EPA will be the responsible agency.

Application of RCRA to Industrial Processes

The **Resource Conservation and Recovery Act (RCRA)** is a law enforced by the EPA that addresses the proper management of **solid waste**, both hazardous and nonhazardous. This law establishes the proper management of hazardous waste from the point of generation through transportation to its final disposal (also known as "cradle-to-grave"), whether it is treatment, storage, or disposal.

RCRA also pertains to the management of nonhazardous solid waste. It establishes the design, location, financial assurance, cleanup, and closure requirements for landfills. The act also prohibits open dumping of solid waste.

RCRA also addresses the hazards associated with **underground storage tanks (UST)** that store petroleum products or other hazardous materials. The threat of USTs is their ability to leak, possibly leading to contamination of groundwater. Depending on the area, groundwater may be a primary source of drinking water for a community. USTs must be permitted and follow other local requirements, such as construction standards, testing, and inspections.

Facilities That Must Obtain Hazardous Waste Permits

The Resource Conservation and Recovery Act (RCRA) was passed to mitigate the impact of hazardous waste and hazardous materials on the environment. It reflects the recognition that **facilities that store, treat, or dispose of hazardous waste** (referred to as "**TSDF**s") present a particular risk to the environment due to the volume and variety of materials at those locations. TSDFs require permits under RCRA. A permit outlines facility design, operations, safety standards, monitoring requirements, and reporting requirements.

Businesses that generate hazardous waste but do not manage it (treat, store, or dispose of) do not require an RCRA permit. If the facility treats its hazardous waste to render it nonhazardous to avoid managing the waste under RCRA, the facility must still apply for an RCRA permit as a TSDF.

RCRA Permit Application Process

When a business opts to construct a new **treatment, storage, and disposal facility** (**TSDF**) for the management of hazardous waste, or when a renewal is due, the facility must apply for a permit. The application process has six steps as follows:

- Public pre-application meeting – The business holds a public meeting to inform the community of the plans for the facility and to obtain any feedback.
- Permit application – A two-part application is submitted that outlines how the facility will protect the environment from its operations, how it will manage emergencies, provisions for environmental cleanups, and closure plans for when the facility is shuttered.
- Permit review – The permitting agency, either a state agency authorized by the EPA to regulate TSDFs or the EPA itself, will review the application.
- **Notice of deficiency (NOD)** issuance – If the application is missing information or is incomplete, an NOD will be issued to the business for correction. This process may take several years due to the complexity of the application.
- Decision – The permitting agency may decide to issue or deny a permit. The decision is conveyed to all who attended the pre-application meeting and is also posted publicly. After a public comment period, the agency may hold a hearing or a hearing can be requested by the public to discuss the decision.
- Final decision – The final decision to approve or deny the permit is made, considering public comments. If the permit is approved, the permitting agency will monitor the construction of the facility to ensure compliance with the permit.

Inspection Requirements for TSDFs

Under the Resource Conservation and Recovery Act (RCRA), the operator of a treatment, storage, and disposal facility (TSDF) must conduct routine inspections of the facility and equipment to identify any potential malfunctions, deteriorations, operator errors, or discharges that could impact the environment. Inspections must occur on a schedule that is written and maintained by the facility. The schedule must also identify what is to be evaluated during each inspection. The operator must review the applicable regulations as the inspection frequency for some operations is designated by standards. For example, loading and unloading areas must be inspected daily while container storage areas must be inspected weekly.

Inspection records must include the date, the time, the name of the inspector, any observations, and the date and scope of any repairs or other corrective actions. The inspection log must be kept for at least three years.

Training Requirements for Personnel at TSDFs

The emphasis of the training program for employees who work at hazardous waste treatment, storage, and disposal facilities (TSDFs) is on emergency response to prevent or halt releases of waste into the environment. Employees must understand the following:

- Emergency equipment and monitoring system inspection, repair, use, and replacement
- The parameters of **automatic waste feed cutoff** equipment
- Alarm systems used at the facility
- How to respond to fires and explosions
- How to respond to groundwater contamination
- How to shut down operations in the event of an emergency

Employees must receive training within six months of starting their position. They can perform supervised work until such time as they receive their training. Refresher training must occur at least annually.

Training Record Requirements for TSDF Employees

Operators of TSDFs must train employees within six months of when they begin to work with hazardous waste at a TSDF and annually thereafter. The training record must log the following:

- Employee name and job title
- Written job description
- Description of the training that is required for each position
- Date of each training

Training records must be kept until the facility is closed or three years after the date an employee leaves the facility.

EPCRA

Emergency Planning and Community Right to Know Act

Passed in 1986 in response to the deadly release of methylisocyanate in Bhopal, India, the **Emergency Planning and Community Right to Know Act (EPCRA)** requires that businesses that store hazardous chemicals or waste inform the community and first responders of the hazards present on-site.

Safety data sheets of certain chemicals must be submitted to state and local agencies as well as to local fire departments to inform them of the materials that are stored on-site and that therefore may be encountered during an emergency response.

EPCRA requires a business to notify the public in the event of a planned or unplanned release of hazardous materials into the environment. Releases must also be reported to the appropriate state and local agencies.

Local governments must have a chemical **emergency response plan (ERP)** in place to manage releases of hazardous materials. If a company possesses an EPA-designated **extremely hazardous substance (EHS)** over the listed **threshold quantity limit (TQL)**, they must participate in the regional planning process.

Businesses that manufacture or consume toxic chemicals, as defined in EPCRA, at or above a TQL must complete an annual **toxic release inventory (TRI)** to monitor their consumption and potential releases of those chemicals.

Extremely Hazardous Substance

A release of any hazardous substance poses a threat to people in and around the point of release. For most substances, planning revolves around how to clean up any spill. However, some chemicals pose a more immediate threat or present a higher degree of hazard if released. These chemicals, termed "extremely hazardous substances (EHS)," pose such a high degree of hazard that emergency planning must include how to prevent releases. The list of EHSs allows communities to prioritize planning for those substances to mitigate the impact on the surrounding community in the event of an emergency. These substances are updated annually in 40 CFR 355, Appendix A.

Criteria for Compliance with EPCRA

A facility must comply with all the provisions of the Environmental Protection and Community Right to Know Act (EPCRA) it meets one of the two following criteria:

- The facility stores or uses an EPA-designated extremely hazardous substance (listed in 40 CFR 355, Appendix A) that exceeds the **threshold planning quantity**
- The facility has been designated for emergency response planning by the State Emergency Response Commission (SERC), state governor, or CEO of the tribe who has jurisdiction of the land.

Reportable Quantity

A **reportable quantity (RQ)** is the designated amount of a given substance under which a release of that substance does not require an emergency response or a notification to the **National Response Center**. For determination purposes, the RQ refers to the total amount of the substance released in any 24-hour period.

The RQ for each of the 600 extremely hazardous substances is listed in the same table as the threshold planning quantity, in 40 CFR 355.

The **Comprehensive Environmental Response, Compensation, and Liability Act (CERCLA)** lists an additional 800 hazardous substances each with an associated RQ. Those RQs are listed in 40 CFR 302.4.

EPA Regulations

Threshold Planning Quantity

The **threshold planning quantity (TPQ)** is a limit for **extremely hazardous substances (EHS)**. Facilities that use or store EHS below the TPQ are not required to abide by the provisions of the Environmental Protection and Community Right to Know Act (EPCRA) while those who manage amounts above the TPQ must comply. The TPQ is not intended to imply a lower risk simply based on volume but will allow communities to prioritize facilities based on the risk they present to the community. The TPQ is simply used to guide comprehensive regional emergency response plans.

Risk Management Plans Under the CAA

Under the **Clean Air Act (CAA)**, the rule regarding **risk management plans (RMPs)** requires that facilities that use or store substances regulated by the CAA above threshold planning quantities (TPQs) must develop plans for industrial accidents. These chemicals and quantities are listed in 42 CFR 7412 (r). This list includes extremely hazardous substances as well as other air pollutants of concern. The RMP must include the following information:

- Any potential effects on the surrounding community of an accident involving an EHS
- Controls the facility has in place to prevent an accident
- Emergency response procedures for accidents involving EHS

RMPs should be provided to local first responders as part of the emergency planning process.

Components

A risk management plan (RMP) when required by the Clean Air Act must have three main sections:

- A section describing the **hazard assessment** of the facility, including the potential effects of any release, a five-year accident history for the facility, and a worst-case accidental release scenario evaluation
- A section outlining the **prevention measures** that are in effect, including safety precautions, maintenance plans, monitoring methods, and employee training
- An emergency response program that includes emergency healthcare provisions, employee emergency response training, and how the facility will notify both first responders and the public in the event of an accident

The RMP must be submitted to the EPA and revised every five years.

SOP

EPA Standard Operating Procedure

A **standard operating procedure (SOP)**, as defined by the Environmental Protection Agency (EPA), is a set of instructions that are used to document activities within an organization that either are routine or occur repeatedly. The intent of the SOP is to ensure that the process or procedure is reproducible and can be properly executed by any member of the organization. Such standardization aids in maintaining the quality and integrity of any end product. The concept of the SOP has been adopted by the EPA to achieve its quality goals.

An SOP can describe either a technical aspect, such as proper sample collection or testing methods, or an administrative aspect, such as audit procedures. The document gives step-by-step processes so that, even in the event of personnel changeover, the processes and the output remain consistent and reliable.

All Environmental Protection Agency (EPA) standard operating procedures have the same five general elements: title page, table of contents, procedures, quality assurance/control, and references. Most of the elements are contained in the body of the SOP.

The title page identifies the name of the process or procedure and includes an identification number, the date of issue or a revision number, the name of the branch that it applies to, and the signatures of the individuals who prepared and approved the document.

The body of the SOP first outlines the purpose of the activity described in the document. The purpose also addresses any applicable regulatory information or standards that the SOP addresses. Next, there is a **definitions section** to provide context for any specialized or unusual terms used in the document. The step-by-step procedures follow the definitions section. These directions are further subdivided into various sections, which can include necessary equipment, personnel qualifications, and any safety considerations. After the directions, the document lists any applicable quality assurance or quality control considerations. The last section of the document lists any applicable references, including citation information for documents that were used to develop the procedure or that are otherwise referenced in the document.

Quality Assurance/Control Section of Technical SOP

A technical standard operating procedure (SOP) instructs users on how to perform a specific **analytical process** in the laboratory or in the field, or how to properly collect samples for future analysis. Technical SOPs may also address data processing, data evaluation, auditing, or conducting risk assessments.

The **quality assurance/control** section of the SOP is critical in ensuring the accuracy and validity of the data as well as the quality and consistency of the activity. This section outlines the necessary equipment checks, such as calibrations and self-checks, as well as quality control (QC) measures (e.g., blanks, controls, replicates, or spikes). These QC measures are used to demonstrate through reports that the instruments and equipment are performing as required and that the output data is as accurate and reliable as the parameters allow. QC data should also include the applicable limits (such as readability and known sources of error) of the method to allow for contextual interpretation of the results.

Shipping and Transporting Materials with Hazards

Hazmat Transportation Requirements

Hazardous Material Shippers and Carriers

In the **Hazardous Materials Transportation Act**, there are references to various parties involved in the movement of hazardous materials and waste. The **shipper** is the entity or person who presents a material for shipping—they are the party who is having the material moved from one location to another. This entity may be a manufacturer shipping to a customer or a waste generator shipping to a waste facility. The **carrier**, sometimes referred to as the **transporter**, is the entity that moves the material or waste from one location to another. The transporter may be a division (e.g., transportation department) within the company that is the shipper, or it may be an outside contractor (e.g., waste hauler). The carrier may operate a ship, truck, train, or aircraft to move material, and each mode of transportation has certain requirements and restrictions that must be understood by the shipper.

Materials Forbidden from Being Shipped

The Hazardous Material Transportation Act (HMTA) specifically forbids the shipment of certain materials, including (but not limited to) the following:

- Batteries and battery-powered devices that can create sparks or generate heat, unless packaged specifically to reduce risk
- Aircraft transportation of materials that generate magnetic fields
- Materials that are incompatible with each other but contained in the same package, where a reaction between the two would generate heat, produce corrosive byproducts, produce flammable vapors, or produce toxic gases
- Materials with a self-accelerating decomposition temperature or self-accelerating polymerization temperature, unless the shipping container is temperature controlled.

Responsibilities of Hazardous Materials Shippers

Under the Hazardous Materials Transportation Act, which is enforced by the Department of Transportation (DOT), the person who offers and prepares hazardous materials for shipment, known as the shipper, has certain responsibilities to ensure the safety of the shipment. Under 49 CFR 173.22, the shipper must do the following:

- Identify the **hazard class** to which the material belongs
- Properly identify the material's **shipping name**
- Package the material using United Nations standard packaging, as required by DOT specifications
- Label and mark the package as to the contents and their associated hazards
- Ensure that the proper **placards** are present on the shipping vehicle
- Verify that the carrier has a permit to ship hazardous materials
- Train personnel on the shipping requirements

In practice, many of these tasks may be executed by the carrier or by the transporter; however, the shipper still must verify that all requirements are met, as the shipper ultimately is the party responsible for the shipment.

Hazmat Packaging, Labeling, and Markings

Dangerous Goods Regulation

The International Air Transport Association (IATA) is a trade association that establishes global standards for the airline industry. IATA has developed the **Dangerous Goods Regulation (DGR)** for the transport of hazardous materials by air. DGR is a United Nations-based standard that has been adopted by the **Federal Aviation Association (FAA)**. Therefore, in the United States, DGR applies to both domestic and international shipments. DGR regulations outline proper packaging, proper labeling, weight/volume limits, and excluded materials. Failure to abide by the regulation can result in a rejected shipment or an enforcement action.

UN Specification Packaging

UN specification packaging refers to international codes for shipping containers that verify that a package configuration (box, barrel, or other type of container) is certified to carry a designated chemical or dangerous good. In the United States, it is a method by which the Department of Transportation ensures that listed materials are packaged in a manner that prevents release during shipment. The UN packaging codes for any specific material are listed in section 14 of the safety data sheet (SDS) for the material.

The packaging codes are alphanumeric and denote the following information about the package to which they apply:

- Type (barrel, drum, box, etc.)
- Material (plastic, aluminum, fiberboard, etc.)
- Category (open or closed top)
- Packing group
- Maximum gross mass or specific gravity
- Solids or inner packaging
- Year of manufacture
- Location of manufacture.

Preparing a Hazardous Substance for Shipping

To ship a hazardous substance, also referred to as a "dangerous good," the shipper must properly prepare and package the substance or material to reduce the risk of a release or accident involving the item. This process can be broken down into seven general steps:

- Step 1 – Determine if the material is a dangerous good by way of its safety data sheet or the UN Dangerous Goods List
- Step 2 – Determine if there are any quantity limits or other shipping restrictions
- Step 3 – Determine if UN specification packaging is required, based on the hazards presented by the material and the quantity of material to be shipped
- Step 4 – Package the material

- Step 5 – Mark and label the package per applicable requirements (i.e., according to the Globally Harmonized System of Classification and Labelling of Chemicals (GHS), Department of Transportation, etc.)
- Step 6 – Complete applicable paperwork and retain necessary copies
- Step 7 – Coordinate shipment with the carrier

UN Packing Groups

Materials classified as dangerous goods for shipment must be properly packaged to reduce the risk of accidents during transport. A material that presents high hazards requires more protecting than a material with a lower risk. For example, a volatile, flammable organic liquid poses a higher fire risk than rolls of paper do. In the UN system, materials are classified as belonging to one of three **packing groups**:

- Packing Group I – Highest risk
- Packing Group II – Medium risk
- Packing Group III – Low risk

Information regarding the packing group for a material is found in section 14 of the safety data sheet. The appropriate packing group can also be found by locating the substance on the Dangerous Goods List, produced by the United Nations Economic Commission for Europe (UNECE).

Labeling and Marking Requirements for Shipping Hazardous Materials

Hazardous materials must be properly labeled to comply with hazard communication regulations. The markings and labels communicate the hazards of the material to those who ship, handle, and transport the items.

Labels and marking for dangerous goods must be in English, must be durable so as to survive the shipping process, must be of a color that contrasts with the packaging in order to be easily visible, cannot be obscured by other markings or labels, and must be located away from any other markings in order to be more clearly visible.

Markings must include the proper shipping name, the UN identification number, handling instructions (such as stacking or lifting requirements), cautions (such as proper orientation to prevent spills), the weight, and any special requirements (including storage temperatures). Radioactive materials, poisons, and limited quantity materials have additional marking requirements. Labels must include hazard classifications that use the Globally Harmonized System of Classification and Labelling of Chemicals (GHS) and Department of Transportation (DOT) hazard classes.

DOT Hazard Classes

Where the Globally Harmonized System of Classification and Labelling of Chemicals (GHS) is an international standard, the US Department of Transportation (DOT) has a parallel system used for the transportation of hazardous materials within the United States. Although the graphics used for similar hazard classes are similar, the US DOT system uses numbers and colors, and uses a slightly different system of classification, as follows:

- **Class 1: Explosives** (orange) – materials that react violently to produce high pressure, which can damage the container and nearby objects or people; divided into six subclasses based on the speed of the reaction

- **Class 2: Gases** (color coded with the applicable colors of other classes if an additional hazard is presented by the material) - compressed gas
- **Class 3: Flammable and combustible liquid** (red) - chemicals in liquid form that can easily ignite
- **Class 4: Flammable solid** (red and white stripes), spontaneously combustible (half red, half white), dangerous when wet (blue) - chemicals in solid form that react with air or water, as well as solid materials that can burn
- **Class 5: Oxidizer and organic peroxide** (yellow) - materials that increase or accelerate burning rates due to the presence of oxygen in their makeup
- **Class 6: Poison** (white, with a skull and crossbones) - toxic materials that can cause illness or death
- **Class 7: Radioactive** (half yellow, half white, with a three-pronged propeller)
- **Class 8: Corrosive** (half white, half black, with hand) - includes acids and bases
- **Class 9: Miscellaneous** (half black and white stripes, half white) - materials that present hazards not covered in any of the other classes

Shipping Papers

Shipping Papers for Hazardous Waste

In general, there are two types of **shipping papers** used for regulated waste transportation—hazardous waste manifests and bills of lading. These documents are not interchangeable and have specific applications.

A **Uniform Hazardous Waste Manifest** is a tracking document required by the Environmental Protection Agency (EPA) and Department of Transportation (DOT) for the shipment of hazardous waste. The document contains a description of the waste, including the amount of waste being shipped and the hazards presented. The manifest is used to demonstrate that the waste was managed properly and that the waste reached its final destination. Copies are retained by parties that handle the waste as a record of adhering to the process.

Shipping Papers for Other Regulated Waste or Hazardous Materials

A **bill of lading (BOL)** is a document used in the shipment of hazardous materials and may be used for other regulated waste, such as medical waste or universal waste. Though a BOL may be used for hazardous materials, it may not be used for hazardous waste. Typically, a BOL does not have the same types of information as a manifest and may be used simply to demonstrate that materials were shipped and who the shipper is.

Requirements for Hazardous Material Shipping Papers

Shipping papers are required as a tracking mechanism for hazardous materials. The papers must include a description of the items, the quantity being shipped, and the number of packages. Each mode (land, sea, and air) has additional requirements as determined by the agency responsible for overseeing the transport. Shipping papers are to ensure that all materials placed in the container arrive at the destination and serve to inform first responders of the potential hazards of the shipped materials if there is an incident during shipment.

If a nonhazardous material is shipped with a dangerous good, the dangerous good must be listed first on the shipping papers, in a different color than the other items, and designated by marking an *X* in the column titled "HM" (hazardous material).

Content Description

When shipping papers are prepared for hazardous materials, regulations require certain information to be included for describing the material. Additionally, the information must be presented in a consistent and specified order. The following information must be present on the shipping papers in the following order:

- The UN number assigned to that material
- The proper shipping name
- The hazard class or division number
- The packing group, expressed in Roman numerals.

For example, muriatic acid would be described on the shipping papers as UN1789, hydrochloric acid, 8, PG II. Information about proper material description can be found in the table in 49 CFR 172.101.

Placarding

Placards

Placards are designated signs, based on the Department of Transportation (DOT) hazard classes, placed on transportation vehicles or shipping containers. They convey the hazards of the materials that are being shipped. Because of the increased risks presented during shipping, the placards serve to warn the public of the hazards when members of the public are near the hazardous material, as when driving. In the event of an accident or a leaking container, the placard informs first responders of the potential hazards, even if first responders are unable to access the shipping papers. Placards are not required when limited amounts of substances are shipped or when infectious substances are being transported.

Requirements for Placarding Hazardous Material Shipments

Hazard class placards are required in specific instances when shipping hazardous materials. The placement of placards is required on bulk packaging, rail cars, freight containers, and transport vehicles. If a transport container holds two or more different hazard categories in non-bulk packages, the container must also be placarded as "dangerous." Materials that are classified as poisons and fall under another hazard class must be placarded with both hazard categories. Placards must be displayed on all four sides of the container as well as the front and back of the vehicle.

Placards are not required when the total amount of hazardous material being shipped is less than one pound or when shipping empty non-bulk containers.

Material Identification Number

The four-digit **material identification number** is required on a transportation placard under specific conditions, including the following:

- when the material is shipped in tank cars, cargo tanks, portable tanks, or other bulk packaging (on two opposite sides of a container under 1,000 gallons and on all four sides of a container over 1,000 gallons)
- when the shipping container holds more than 4,000 kg (8,820 pounds) of non-bulk packages of a single hazardous material
- when more than 1,000 kg (2,205 pounds) of non-bulk containers of inhalation poison materials are being shipped

In any of these three conditions, the shipping container can be shown on the DOT classification placard, or it can be on a separate placard that uses black lettering on an orange field or black lettering on a white placard.

Hazard Classes That Must Be Placarded for Any Quantity of Material

In general, placarding is required when a large amount of material is being shipped. However, some substances present such hazards that they must be placarded whenever any quantity of them is shipped. These six classes (located in Table 1 of 49 CFR 172.504) include:

- Class 1 explosives
- Poison gases
- Water-reactive chemicals
- Organic peroxides
- Inhalation poisons
- Radioactive materials

Removing Placards from Emptied Bulk Containers

Tanks, tanker cars, and bulk containers must be placarded to convey the hazard that the material they contain presents to carriers or the public. Placards are required on bulk containers that contain or have contained hazardous materials. There are three instances when a placard can be removed from an emptied bulk container:

- if the container is cleaned and purged so that no residue of the hazardous material remains
- if the container is filled with a non-hazardous material
- if the container is filled with a material of a different hazard class, in which case the removed placard must be replaced with one that reflects the new material

Accepting and Rejecting Shipments

Rejecting Shipments

A generator of hazardous waste must have a relationship with the treatment, storage, and disposal facility (TSDF) to make sure that their shipment is not rejected upon arrival. A TSDF may reject a shipment because of restrictions on their permit (they do not have the proper facilities or equipment to manage the waste), capacity limitations, or other reasons, such as improper packaging or incorrect labeling. A shipment may be rejected in part or in whole, and rejection must be communicated to the generator.

Process When TSDF Rejects Hazardous Waste Shipments

If a treatment, storage, and disposal facility (TSDF) partially or wholly rejects a shipment of hazardous waste, they must consult with the generator on next steps. The decision may be to transfer the waste to another TSDF or to return the waste to the generator. This decision is ultimately the responsibility of the generator. If the transporter is still on site, the TSDF will amend the Uniform Hazardous Waste Manifest by completing the **alternate destination facility** section. The TSDF retains a copy of the manifest and sends the other copies with the waste to the new facility or back to the generator. If the TSDF rejects only part of the shipment and the transporter has left, the TSDF creates a new manifest to use for shipping the waste to another permitted facility or back to the generator.

Process When TSDF Accepts Hazardous Waste Shipment

When a shipment of hazardous waste arrives at a treatment, storage, and disposal facility (TSDF), the facility must determine if they will accept or reject the shipment. If they accept the shipment, this means that their facility can manage the material properly. The TSDF then determines if there are any discrepancies between the manifest and the shipment. If no discrepancies are identified, then the facility will enter a **management method code** on the manifest next to each container. The facility designee then signs the manifest, acknowledging receipt of the waste. The facility will retain a copy of the manifest and send the fully signed original to the generator, demonstrating that the waste process was successfully completed. (At the end of this process, the generator should have two copies of every manifest.) The state agency that is responsible for hazardous waste management may also require a signed copy from the TSDF that can be used to cross-check the process.

Storing Materials with Hazards

Hazmat Storage Location Site Requirements

Hazards Associated with Improper Hazardous Material Storage

The improper storage of hazardous materials can result in accidental releases and exposures of not only employees but also, when large volumes or extremely hazardous materials are involved, surrounding communities. Storage of organic solvents, organic peroxides, or flammable gases presents a flammability hazard. Some materials are classified as explosives, which present not only a flammability hazard but also an associated destructive **overpressure hazard**. Compressed gas cylinders present high-pressure hazards that can result in a release of gas over a large area. Also, in the event the cylinder itself is damaged, the cylinder can become a projectile. When multiple chemicals are stored in close proximity, there is the hazard of an unintended reaction that can cause a fire, explosion, toxic byproduct, or other negative result. Some chemicals must be prevented from exposure to air while others react violently with water. Other chemicals will react with solvents or other fuels to spontaneously start fires that will self-propagate.

General Requirements for Hazardous Material or Hazardous Waste Storage Areas

Hazardous chemicals and hazardous waste can present a variety of hazards in the workplace, including toxicity, corrosion, and flammability. However, proper storage of these materials can reduce the risk of realizing a hazard. Properly designed storage areas will reduce the chances of employee exposure and the chances of chemical incidents.

Chemicals should be protected from precipitation and direct sunlight, both of which may cause releases. Storage areas should have proper **ventilation** to allow vapors and gases to escape, maintaining a safe environment within which employees can operate. Ventilation systems may be powered by gravity or be mechanical, but they must allow for fresh air to enter to reduce the risk of a toxic or flammable atmosphere forming. Buildings should be designed specifically for the materials they will contain, as flammable and explosive materials have specific storage requirements, including **fire-rated construction**. Spill control mechanisms (such as drainage systems, dikes, berms, or basins) must be integral to the storage area. Impermeable floors are required for these storage areas, to prevent liquids from seeping into the soil. If a single storage area is to be used, it must be constructed with adequate space to allow for the proper separation and segregation of incompatible materials.

Hazardous Material Separation and Hazardous Material Segregation

To prevent reactions between incompatible chemicals, hazardous materials should be properly separated and segregated. In this context, **segregation** means to assign a substance to a particular hazard group. This allows chemicals that have similar hazards to each other but that will not react with one another to be safely stored together. **Separation**, for hazardous materials storage, involves providing either physical or spatial barriers between incompatible materials. For example, flammable gases should be separated from oxygen cylinders by way of a fire-resistant wall or by at least 20 feet. By utilizing the concepts of segregation and separation, a single facility can allow for the safe storage of a variety of chemicals.

Safety Items

Chemical storage areas present a high risk due to because they tend to be relatively small spaces containing either a large amount of chemicals or a variety of chemicals. Thus, to increase the safety of employees, each chemical storage area should have access to a **spill kit**, a fire extinguisher, and a safety shower or eyewash apparatus. The fire extinguisher and safety shower should be exterior to the storage area but within such a distance that an employee can quickly reach them. The spill kit should be adequate and appropriate, in both size and materials, for the substances contained in the storage area. The fire extinguisher should also be appropriate for the chemicals in the storage area, and consideration should be given to whether a combination extinguisher is necessary.

Requirements for TSDF Hazardous Waste Storage Areas

The Environmental Protection Agency (EPA) establishes requirements for **containment areas** used to store hazardous waste at a permitted treatment, storage, and disposal facility (TSDF). The containment system is intended to prevent the release of waste into the environment if there is a leak or spill. The storage area must meet the following requirements:

- Have an impermeable floor without cracks or seams and having a raised curb or berm to contain liquid spills (not required in storage areas holding only solid materials)
- Have a floor that is sloped or otherwise designed so that spilled fluids can be collected and removed
- Have a spill collection capacity of greater than either 10 percent of the total volume of material stored in the area or 100 percent of the largest container being stored
- Have a system to prevent stormwater from entering the storage area, or have a collection system for runoff to prevent contaminated stormwater from entering the environment
- Have a system to notify an operator of a spill or leak so that the material can be removed in a timely manner

Ignition Control Measures in Areas That Contain Flammable Chemicals

Fires require three elements (known as the "fire triangle")—fuel, oxygen, and an energy source. The removal of any one element will prevent a fire from starting. When flammable chemicals or waste are present, they provide the fuel, and storage areas typically have adequate oxygen for combustion. Thus, the best method of preventing fire would be to eliminate any sources of energy or ignition in storage areas.

Signs and policies that prohibit smoking and open flames in flammable chemical storage areas will remove human-based ignition sources. All fixtures, including lights, pumps, and mechanical ventilation equipment, must be rated for flammable atmospheres to reduce any electrical sparks. Finally, any high-temperature equipment must be physically separated from these storage areas to reduce their impact on flammable and combustible materials.

Requirements for Tanks Storing Bulk Amounts of Flammable Liquids

Due to the hazards of fire and explosion associated with the bulk storage of flammable liquids, the **Occupational Safety and Health Administration (OSHA)** has established strict guidelines for tanks that hold these materials. The preferred material for above-ground tanks is steel, but other suitable materials may be used, as long as they meet the **Underwriters Laboratories** standard for aboveground tank construction. Additionally, aboveground tanks must be spaced at least three feet apart. Spacing must be greater when there are three or more rows of tanks, to allow for firefighter access. Tanks must be vented to prevent the buildup of pressure from evaporating liquid as well as have **emergency venting** in the event of a fire inside the tank. OSHA also outlines the drainage and dike systems for aboveground tanks. Underground tanks must be installed at least one foot from any structure and three feet from any property line. Underground tanks must be covered with at least six inches of soil and must have a corrosion protection system.

Requirements for Hazardous Chemical Storage Cabinets

Proper storage of hazardous chemicals can reduce the risk of accidents and reactions between incompatible materials. Storage cabinets must be constructed of materials compatible with the contents, meaning corrosives should not be stored in metal cabinets and flammable chemicals should be kept out of wooden cabinets. Cabinets should be properly **fire-rated** for the materials they contain and should be routinely inspected to make sure they remain in good condition. Storage areas for corrosives should allow for bases to be separated from acids, allow for oxidizing acids to be separated from other chemicals, and provide **secondary containment** for drips and spills. Flammable cabinets should be vented to prevent vapors from concentrating inside. All chemical storage cabinets should have doors that close and can be secured to prevent unauthorized access.

Inventory of Hazardous Chemicals

An inventory of hazardous chemicals serves to inform employees about which substances are present and to inform regulatory or first responder agencies of the materials that are on site.

Under the **Hazard Communication Standard**, an employer who has hazardous chemicals on site must prepare a written hazard communication program to inform employees of those hazards. As part of this program, the employer must compile a list of all hazardous chemicals on site.

The Emergency Planning and Community Right to Know Act (EPCRA) requires that every business provide an inventory to local response agencies if they maintain regulated substances above the threshold quantity. Providing an inventory to these agencies allows them to plan for releases and emergencies at the facility.

Hazardous Materials Signage and Labelling Requirements

Signage Identifying Hazardous Materials and Waste Storage Locations

Signs that are required for identifying hazardous chemical storage areas and hazardous waste storage areas must abide by National Fire Prevention Association (NFPA) **Hazardous Material Code**. Signs must comply with applicable codes and must be in English. Supplemental language signs are allowed, but signs in English are required. Signs must be protected from damage as they must remain legible to notify employees of the hazards within. Signs must be weather-resistant, which can be challenging in instances where color-coding is required by a standard. Housekeeping must ensure that signs are visible at all times. If a sign becomes worn, faded, or illegible, it must be replaced.

Facilities must also comply with any additional local or state signage requirements for these storage locations.

National Fire Prevention Association 704

Signage System

The **National Fire Prevention Association (NFPA) 704** standard is a hazardous material labeling system that is designed to provide information to first responders. The system is based on a color code for hazard categories (blue, yellow, red, and white) as well as a numeric rating system. The numeric hazard rating system is a 0 through 4 rating, with 0 representing the lowest risk and 4 representing the highest.

The system is designed to quickly convey general information to fire and police departments who may be responding to an emergency involving the labeled substances. The color-coding and number system relays such information as whether respiratory protection will be required, the degree of flammability, and whether water should be used to extinguish a fire or if that could make the situation worse.

Color-Coding System

The National Fire Prevention Association (NFPA) 704 labeling system uses color-coded diamonds with numerals. The diamond is constructed from four smaller diamonds that fit together, with a blue diamond on the left, a red diamond on top, a yellow diamond on the right, and a white diamond on bottom:

- Blue is the rating for health hazards. Health hazards can vary from skin irritation to organ-specific toxins to toxic materials.
- Red is the rating for flammability.
- Yellow is the rating for stability or reactivity.
- White is for special precautions. Although a variety of symbols may be shown here, NFPA recognizes only three—W for water reactive chemicals, OX for oxidizers, and SA for simple asphyxiant gases.

Number Rating System for the Blue, Red, and Yellow Diamonds

The numerical rating in the NFPA 704 system provides an assessment of the level of danger presented by the labeled chemical in each of three categories—health, flammability, and stability/reactivity. Each category is rated from 0 to 4, with 0 presenting no hazard and 4 presenting an extreme hazard. The ratings for each category are as follows:

- Health (blue) -
  - 0 represents no hazard;
  - 1 means an exposure would result in a mild reaction or injury;
  - 2 means the chemical may cause temporary incapacitation or other residual injury over prolonged exposures;
  - 3 signifies that the substance causes temporary or residual injury over short exposures; a level 4 material can cause serious injury or death with short exposures
- Flammability (red) -
  - 0-rated chemicals are not flammable;
  - 1-rated chemicals require heating in order to burn (flash points greater than 200 degrees Fahrenheit, combustible);
  - 2 indicates that the chemical has a flash points between 100 and 200 degrees Fahrenheit;
  - 3-rated materials will ignite under normal conditions and have flash points lower than 100 degrees Fahrenheit;
  - 4 is used for chemicals that readily burn and have flash points below normal room temperature (70 degrees Fahrenheit)

- Reactivity/stability (yellow) -
  - 0 means the chemical is very stable;
  - 1-rated chemicals are normally stable but may become unstable at high temperatures or pressures;
  - 2 means the substance may have violent reactions at high pressure or temperatures or may be water reactive;
  - 3 indicates that the material can detonate or explode when exposed to heat, water, or shock;
  - 4-rated chemicals can react or detonate under normal conditions

Locations Where Labels are Required

The National Fire Prevention Association (NFPA) Hazardous Materials Code identifies four locations that should have NFPA 704 labels to inform first responders and others of the hazards present in an area or vessel. These locations are the following:

- Stationary aboveground tanks
- Stationary aboveground containers
- Entrances or locations where hazardous materials or waste is stored, dispensed, used, or handled in quantities that require a permit
- Any other location where a local authority has determined a label is necessary

Labeling Requirements

Hazardous Materials Containers

The intent of a hazardous material label is to convey safety and health information to the user. For any given material, the label provides a quick summary of hazards, health effects, and precautions that should be taken. Labeling requirements are established in the Occupational Safety and Health Administration (OSHA) **Hazard Communication Standard**, which is based on the United Nations' Globally Harmonized System of Classification and Labelling of Chemicals. A material that is classified as hazardous must be labeled with a product identifier, **signal word**, **hazard statements,** **pictograms**, **precautionary statements**, and **manufacturer information**.

Hazardous Waste Containers

The waste generator is responsible for the proper labeling of hazardous waste containers that they will offer for transport. Each container that is less than 119 gallons must be labeled with the following:

- The words "Hazardous Waste - Federal Law Prohibits Improper Disposal. If found, contact the nearest police or public safety authority or the US Environmental Protection Agency."
- The generator's name and address
- The generator's EPA identification number
- The manifest tracking number (when the container is listed on a manifest for shipment to a management facility)
- EPA hazardous waste code numbers

The generator should be aware that state agencies may require different or additional information to be shown on waste container labels.

Hazardous Materials/Waste Access Control

Materials Required to Be Secured from Unauthorized Access

The National Fire Prevention Association (NFPA) has identified six types of substances that, when present in bulk amounts, require additional security. These types of substances are as follows:

- Unpackaged organic peroxides that explosively decompose
- Class 3 and Class 4 oxidizers
- **Pyrophoric** chemicals
- Class 3 and Class 4 reactive chemicals that are unstable
- Highly toxic materials
- Water-reactive liquids

NFPA requires that the storage, handling, dispensing, and use areas at the facility be secured against unauthorized entry. The intent of this requirement is to prevent persons from stealing the materials or initiating them, resulting in a large-scale chemical emergency.

Security Measures to Limit Access to Hazardous Materials

Storage areas containing hazardous materials are at risk of being accessed by unauthorized personnel who may be looking for chemicals to produce chemical bombs or weapons, or for other illegal uses. Sites that have chemicals, particularly chemicals that are susceptible to **diversion**, should implement measures to limit access to chemical stores.

Keeping storage areas locked and issuing keys only to specific individuals will reduce the number of people who have access. Logs that track who accesses chemical stores as well as an inventory tracking system can reduce the risk of chemicals being removed from the inventory without permission. Security cameras can monitor activities in the storage area 24 hours a day while staffed storerooms limit the general access to chemical stores. Areas where hazardous materials are stored can have an additional security fence to prevent unauthorized access. The perimeter of the facility should also be secured to prevent public access to storage locations and to equipment that transports materials throughout the facility.

Determining Whether Storage Areas Meet Applicable Standards

Routine, periodic inspections should be conducted to determine whether a storage area meets standards and requirements for safety. Inspections should verify that signage is present and appropriate, required safety equipment is available and in good condition, and all **engineering controls** are in place and functioning. Materials should be properly labeled, hazard classes properly segregated, and incompatible materials properly separated. Inspections should be documented, and any corrective actions should be taken if necessary to ensure chemicals are safely and properly stored.

Facility Operations Involving Materials with Hazards

Engineering Controls

The treatment of hazardous waste may generate heat, pressure, toxic gases, or violent reactions. Thus, the content and **chemical profile** of the waste must be understood to prevent reactions that can be hazardous to employee health or damage the facility. Local exhaust ventilation over the treatment processes or enclosing the reaction vessel will reduce the chance of hazardous vapors escaping. **Neutralization reactions** or other treatment processes that generate heat can have cooling jackets or other heat removal systems to reduce the risk of a violent reaction. Controlling the addition of treatment chemicals or wastes to be combined will also allow for better control of heat or gases produced. If the treatment process generates flammable vapors, those can be directed to a **flare unit** to prevent their release into the environment.

Controls to Prevent or Contain Hazardous Chemical Spills

By implementing measures to contain and control spills, the employer can reduce the risk of environmental damage, employee injuries, and fiscal penalties. Plastic spill skids and pallets can be used to store large volumes of hazardous materials. These devices have hollow bottoms to capture any leaking material and prevent it from contacting the ground or entering drains. Alternatives can include portable spill containment berms to store chemicals. All drains near storage areas should be covered or otherwise protected from fluids entering them using drain covers, seals, or socks. Employees should be trained on proper storage and handling of chemicals as well as what to do in the event that a spill occurs or a leak is noticed. Storage areas should be inspected regularly to make sure containers are in good condition, control measures are being used, and containers are not leaking.

Engineering Controls for Hazardous Waste Storage Areas

The safe storage of hazardous waste requires that the specific characteristics of the waste be understood to prevent accidents. When the profile of the waste is understood, engineering controls can be implemented for storage locations. Flammable materials should be stored in areas that have proper ventilation. Such areas should also be free of ignition sources, as when **intrinsically safe lighting** is used. Fire-resistant enclosures will prevent the spread of any fire that starts inside and prevent any external fire from accessing the fuel in the storage location. Materials that are incompatible with each other, such as oxidizers and flammables, must be separated with physical barriers or distance. **Secondary containment**, such as double-wall tanks or catch basins, should be used whenever possible to contain potential leaks or spills.

Controls for Disposal

The most common method of disposal of hazardous waste is permanent internment in specially designed **landfills**. To be permitted for hazardous waste, the landfill must have the following features:

- A double-lined bottom
- **Leachate** collection systems
- Leak detection systems to protect nearby groundwater

- Stormwater run-on and runoff systems to prevent rainwater from leaching into the waste
- A **cap** of at least 12 inches of soil when at capacity, and an additional leachate collection system installed in the cap

Process Training Record Requirements

Required Components of Employee Training Under the PSM Standard

Process safety management (PSM) is a program that is required for facilities that use, manage, store, or handle extremely hazardous materials. The Occupational Safety and Health Administration (OSHA) promotes effective training as a means of improving employee safety. Thus, OSHA has established training requirements under process safety to decrease the risk of catastrophic events involving hazardous substances. The training required under the PSM standard consists of three components:

- Initial training
- Refresher training that must occur every three years after the initial training
- Training documentation that records that the employee received the training, that they understood the material, and the method through which employee understanding was determined and evaluated

Initial Training Program Topics Required Under the PSM Standard

Employees who are currently part of, or are newly assigned, to a process involving extremely hazardous substances must undergo initial training under the Occupational Health and Safety Administration (OSHA) process safety management (PSM) regulation. Initial training must address the specific safety and health hazards of the substances the employee will be working with, actions to take in an emergency (including proper shutdown procedures to prevent compounding of the situation), and safe work practices for the employee's job.

Hazcom Requirements for SDS

Required Elements of Hazard Communication Programs

A **hazard communication program** is intended to establish a system wherein employees are informed of the risks associated with the chemicals they may encounter on the job. Such a program requires employers to inform their employees of the hazards presented by the chemicals they work with, how to identify the hazards associated with any particular substance, and what **protective measures** are available to reduce the risk of an exposure. The employer must have a written hazard communication ("hazcom") program that addresses the following:

- proper labeling or other forms of warnings
- how safety data sheets will be managed and made available to employees
- how employee training will be conducted

Hazard Communication Label Information

Section 1 of Safety Data Sheet

A safety data sheet consists of 16 standardized sections. The contents of each section are designated by the Globally Harmonized hazard communication system (GHS). Per GHS requirements, section 1 contains identification information. This section contains the product name, including its technical name, scientific name, and trade names, as well as other synonyms. This section also contains information on both the recommended and restricted uses of the material. Also required is the supplier information, including name, address, and contact telephone number. The last piece of information required in this section is a phone number that can be used in emergencies for additional information about the substance.

Section 2 of Safety Data Sheet

The format and content of a safety data sheet (SDS) is designated, under the Hazard Communication Standard, by the Globally Harmonized System (GHS) of hazard communication. Section 2 is designated for hazards identification. This section contains the GHS hazard classification of the substance, including the GHS hazard rating. Other information in section 2 includes the signal word, hazard statements and codes, precautionary statements and codes, and GHS pictograms. This information is required by the Hazard Communication Standard to be on container labels.

PPE for Sampling and Handling

Chemical Protective Ensemble

A **chemical protective ensemble** is made up of pieces of **personal protective equipment (PPE)** and protects the entire body. A chemical protective suit is selected to protect the arms, legs, and body from chemical exposure. Suits may be separate pieces, or they can have booties and hoods attached. The feet are protected by chemical resistant boots, which typically extended above the calf to protect from any splashes. Boots may have steel shanks to provide puncture protection for the soles of the feet. Chemical-resistant gloves are worn (sometimes multiple pairs) to protect the hands. The face can be protected by a **full-face respirator** or, if allowed, a **half-face respirator** and **chemical splash goggles**. Finally, to protect the head from injury, a hard hat can be worn.

Levels of Protective Clothing Ensembles

Chemical clothing ensembles are described in levels from A to D, with Level D offering the least protection and Level A providing the most. This standardized system allows employers and employees to understand what pieces of personal protective equipment are required and what relative level of hazards is expected:

- **Level D** (nuisance hazards): typical work uniform of a shirt, pants, and work boots (or safety shoes); may also include the use of an uncoated protective garment to keep the clothes clean
- **Level C** (airborne hazards present, but known; skin and eye hazards unlikely): a work uniform underneath other garments; can include an uncoated or coated protective garment as well as respiratory protection by way of an air-purifying respirator (full-face, half-face with goggles, or a **powered air-purifying respirator**); will include a coated protective garment as well as chemical resistant gloves (typically an inner pair and an outer pair) when liquid or gaseous chemicals are present
- **Level B** (higher level of respiratory protection): uses the same equipment as Level C but has a coated garment and the respirator is a supplied-air type (either a **self-contained breathing apparatus** or an **airline respirator**)
- **Level A** (highest level of protection, unknown atmospheres, skin-absorbing chemicals, uncontrolled releases): a Level B ensemble is worn underneath a fully encapsulating suit; requires specialized training

Recommended Protective Equipment

On a GHS-compliant safety data sheet (SDS), section 8 is to contain exposure control methods, which includes recommended personal protective equipment (PPE). Typically, an SDS will have separate information for skin, eye, and respiratory protection measures. Information may include whether protective measures are recommended and under what circumstances (e.g., "when high concentrations are present"). The SDS usually will not state the specific type of equipment required, such as the best material for the chemical resistant glove.

Hazmat Testing Procedures

Hazards and Risks

"Hazard" and "risk" are two terms that are often confused but have different meanings. A hazard is the inherent ability of a substance to do harm. The hazard is present whenever the material is present, regardless of amount. For example, toluene is always flammable regardless of whether there is only a teaspoon present or an entire tanker truck. Risk the probability under a specific set of circumstances that the hazard will be realized and impact workers or the environment. Toluene is always flammable but will only catch fire when exposed to an ignition source. Thus, using intrinsically safe lighting fixtures reduces the risk of fire wherever toluene is stored.

Determining Potential Hazards of Materials

The Hazard Communication Standard (HazCom) applies only to chemicals that are determined to be hazardous. The process of determining whether a chemical is hazardous is referred to as "**hazard determination**."

Under the Occupational Safety and Health Administration (OSHA) guidance document for HazCom, the entity responsible for bringing the chemical into the United States (i.e., the importer or manufacturer) must make the determination as to whether a substance is hazardous and provide such information to the end user by way of the safety data sheet and labeling.

A hazard determination evaluates both the physical and health hazards of a material. Physical hazards include flammability or reactivity while health hazards include carcinogenicity or organ toxicity. Information is gathered and interpreted from available scientific information and resources. For chemical manufacturers, some of this information may be determined by way of in-house testing.

Hazard Determination for Substances

Only hazardous substances fall under the scope of the HazCom standard. The process of hazard determination follows a four-step process:

- Selection of the material – The manufacturer or importer must first determine what material, chemical, or preparation will be evaluated for its potential hazards. Selection includes an assessment of whether the substance is exempt and, if not, if relevant data already exists.
- Data collection – Relevant data is collected from references or resources, or by conducting testing.
- Data analysis – The data is analyzed and compared to thresholds, criteria, or definitions to determine if the product presents a particular hazard that requires specific labeling and notification for the end user.
- Documentation – The procedures used in hazard determination must be recorded along with the data used to make the determination. Ultimately, this information will be used to prepare a safety data sheet for the material.

Physical Hazard

One of the two categories that must be evaluated for a chemical is physical hazard. A **physical hazard** is one that causes harm upon contact with the body. Under the Hazard Communication Standard, physical hazards include flammable substances, combustible liquid, compressed gas, explosives, organic peroxides, oxidizers, pyrophoric (air-reactive) substances, instability (reactive substances), and water-reactive substances. Under the Globally Harmonized System of Classification and Labelling of Chemicals, physical hazard classes include explosives, flammables, oxidizers, and gases under pressure.

Health Hazards

The Occupational Safety and Health Administration (OSHA) describes the other of the two hazard categories for a substance as the impact on employee health. Chemicals that present **health hazards** impact one or more organ systems of the body based on short- or long-term exposure. A chemical may cause harm to any body part that it contacts, such as an acid damaging an eye, or it may be organ-specific, such as ethanol targeting the liver. Under the Hazard Communications Standard, health hazards include carcinogens, toxic materials, reproductive toxins, irritants, corrosives, sensitizers, hepatotoxins, nephrotoxins, neurotoxins, blood system toxins (toxins that target the hematopoietic system), respiratory irritants, chemicals that damage the eyes, and chemicals that attach to the mucous membranes. The Globally Harmonized System of Classification and Labelling of Chemicals health hazards include corrosivity, toxicity, and irritation.

Categories of Data Required to Determine Whether Chemicals are Hazardous

To determine whether a chemical is hazardous, data must be collected. All physical and health hazards associated with a material must be identified so that the hazard can be conveyed to the end users. The three categories of data needed to identify a hazard are as follows:

- **Chemical identity** – includes the technical name, common names, synonyms, Chemical Abstracts Services (CAS) number, and any other identifier that provides information on the contents or composition
- Physical and chemical properties – includes information such as physical appearance, boiling point, melting point, flash point, and solubility
- Health effects – involves evaluating the substance to determine if it meets the criteria for any of the 14 health hazards listed under the Hazard Communication Standard

Evaluation of Chemical's Hazardous Properties

The evaluation of a chemical for its **hazardous potential** requires the manufacturer or importer to collect data in three categories—chemical identity, physical and chemical properties, and health effects.

Identity information is in section 1 of the safety data sheet (SDS), with the Chemical Abstract Services (CAS) number being listed in section 3 (Composition/Ingredients). Section 9 is titled Physical and Chemical Properties and contains all known data that can assist in the evaluation of such things as inhalation potential and how a material will react when it comes into contact with water. Health effects are listed in section 11, and this list will include effects on eyes, skin, and respiratory system. This section may also contain any published exposure limits.

Security at Sites Managing Hazardous Materials

Sites that use or store hazardous materials or process hazardous waste are susceptible to accidental and intentional site access. People or animals may unintentionally access the site and can put themselves in danger, damage equipment, or otherwise create a liability. Persons looking to do harm by stealing hazardous materials for illicit uses or to cause a chemical incident by initiating a release can put others in danger. Thus, a site should take proper security precautions. The facility must put in place a 24-hour monitoring system (such as one that uses cameras or guards) or erect a barrier to limit access to the facility. In addition, areas where materials are being stored, treated, or otherwise used on the facility grounds must be marked with signs warning of the danger.

Disposition of Materials with Hazards

Waste Profile Components

Identifying a Substance as Hazardous Waste

The Environmental Protection Agency (EPA) has developed a process to determine if a substance is a hazardous waste and must therefore be managed under the Resource Conservation and Recovery Act (RCRA). To determine if a material must be managed as a hazardous waste, the person or company that generates the waste must:

- Step 1: designate the material as waste, having no further purpose for the user and being neither reusable nor recyclable
- Step 2: identify the material as a solid waste that requires management
- Step 3: determine if the waste is excluded under RCRA (as specific items and processes have exclusions)
- Step 4: identify whether the substance is a listed waste under RCRA, which establishes specific materials, byproducts, and products from certain industries and processes as hazardous wastes
- Step 5: determine if the waste exhibits specific hazardous characteristics, such as corrosivity, toxicity, reactivity, or flammability
- Step 6: evaluate state regulations to determine if the substance must be managed properly even though it may not meet the federal definition of a hazardous waste.

If an unwanted material goes through the process and is determined not to be hazardous, other evaluations must be undertaken to determine if the waste falls under other regulations (as in the case of universal waste or medical waste) or whether it is unregulated and can go to local municipal landfills.

Hazardous Waste Profile

A **hazardous waste profile**, also referred to as a "**characterization profile**," is a description of the physical and chemical properties of a waste product. These properties are evaluated to determine the hazard or hazards presented by the waste. Hazardous waste can be characterized as corrosive (pH less than or equal to 2 or greater than or equal to 12.5), **ignitable** (liquid and having a flash point less than 140 degrees Fahrenheit), reactive with air or water, or meeting the criteria for toxicity. The waste profile also describes other aspects of the waste, such as **heavy metal** content, specific **ions** such as lead or arsenic, and any **radioactive** components.

The knowledge of these characteristics will determine how the waste is to be managed. The profile is used to properly package the material and separate it from other materials that could increase the risk of an incident during transport. Additionally, the profile will determine whether a waste-handling facility can receive the waste, based on their permitted activities. Hazardous waste receiving sites cannot accept waste that is not accompanied by a profile.

Creating a Profile

The generator of hazardous waste is responsible for creating an accurate characterization profile of the material. The generator may rely on one of two methods to profile a waste product—laboratory analysis or knowledge of the waste.

In the laboratory method, the waste is analyzed, and the results are used to identify what, if any, hazardous characteristics the waste exhibits. Testing includes determining the pH for corrosivity, using toxicity testing methods, and doing instrumental analysis for flash point, heavy metal content, and other aspects of the waste.

As an alternative to testing, the generator may use knowledge of the materials that went into the waste to characterize the material. In this method, the generator assesses the physical and chemical properties of the materials that went into the process to determine the potential hazard of the waste.

Required Information

The waste profile is a description of the waste that provides information to the treatment, storage, and disposal facility (TSDF) regarding management strategies. The waste profile must describe the waste in such a way that the TSDF can develop a plan to verify the characteristics and contents. The profile should include the following information:

- The common name of the waste material
- A description of the process that generated the waste
- Source and form codes provided by the Environmental Protection Agency
- Whether the waste is a material that is regulated by the Department of Transportation
- A physical description of the waste material
- Physical properties including odor, physical state, number of liquid phases, pH, and flash point
- Resource Conservation and Recovery Act waste codes
- State waste codes, if required by the state agency
- A percentage breakdown of the chemical composition of the material
- Any other categories that would include the waste, such as explosive, shock-sensitive, pyrophoric, compressed gases, heavy metals, asbestos, medical waste, and ammonia-containing compounds

Waste Analysis Plan

To determine the appropriate disposition of a waste, a treatment, storage, and disposal facility (TSDF) must analyze all waste that it receives. This process is used to ensure that the facility can accept and manage the waste and that the waste does not need to be transferred to another facility. Additionally, it verifies the waste profile so that the waste is stored and treated properly. The profile is assessed by the TSDF's **waste analysis plan (WAP)**. The WAP must include the following:

- What parameters (characteristics or physical properties) of the waste will be analyzed
- The testing and analytical methods that will be used to collect data
- How a representative sample will be determined and collected, including how many are required
- How often the waste must be re-evaluated during its management
- Whether waste analyses from the generator will be accepted, what analyses will be accepted, and how these analyses will be evaluated
- How the TSDF will verify that the waste received matches the waste shipped as stated on the manifest

Waste Disposal Options

Land Disposal Restriction Program for Hazardous Waste

As part of the **Hazardous and Solid Waste Amendments (HSWA)** for the Resource Conservation and Recovery Act (RCRA), Congress created the **Land Disposal Restriction (LDR)** program. LDR requires that any solid hazardous waste must be treated before it is disposed of in a permitted landfill. The goal of this restriction is to prevent or reduce the amount of contaminants that **leach** into groundwater from land disposal facilities. Thus, the generator must identify whether the waste they generate will be sent to a land disposal facility. If so, the generator is subject to the LDR program.

The generator must determine whether the waste is listed in the treatment standards table found in 40 CFR 268.40. If so, the generator must ensure that the waste meets the criteria listed on the table before presenting the waste for shipment to a land disposal facility.

Determining How Waste Must Be Treated

To determine whether the waste must be treated pursuant to the Land Disposal Restriction (LDR) program, the generator must first characterize the waste. After the characterization is completed, the generator must assign the proper Environmental Protection Agency (EPA**) waste codes** to the waste. The code for the waste is then cross-referenced with the LDR treatment tables. These tables denote which chemicals in the waste must be treated, how those chemicals must be treated, and the maximum allowable residual concentration of the chemicals after treatment.

Characteristic wastes can be treated to the degree that they no longer meet the criteria of hazardous waste. Such methods (termed "**decharacterization** processes") are listed by the EPA for each hazard class.

TSDF

A treatment, storage, and disposal facility (TSDF) is the final stop for hazardous waste that is shipped by a generator. In the **cradle-to-grave** concept, the TSDF is typically the "grave" for hazardous waste. TSDFs undergo separate, intensive permitting processes as they are the final destination for hazardous waste and are responsible for keeping the waste from entering the environment. A TSDF may have **incineration, encapsulation, recycling,** or **landfill** options for waste. Not all TSDFs can accept all wastes, and it is the responsibility of the generator to determine whether the waste they are shipping can be received at a particular TSDF.

Treatment of Hazardous Waste

Hazardous waste can be treated or disposed of as methods of management. Same waste categories, such as those that have land disposal restrictions (LDRs), must be treated prior to disposal. "Hazardous waste treatment" refers to any process that changes the physical, chemical, or biological properties of waste to render it either nonhazardous or less hazardous. Processes include **neutralization, oxidation, reduction,** and **heat treatment**. Treatment also includes methods of recovering energy or material resources from the waste or volume reduction strategies, such as evaporation or combustion. If the end-product of treatment is nonhazardous, it can be managed as unregulated waste. If the end product is hazardous, it must be sent to a permitted landfill for permanent storage.

Storage Facility and Transfer Facility

A treatment, storage, and disposable facility (TSDF) may be the final destination for hazardous waste, or it may be an intermediary. A TSDF may store hazardous materials, storage being defined by the Environmental Protection Agency as holding the material for a short time before treatment, disposal, or transfer. Storage may include an on-site area for holding the waste before moving it to another location at the same facility or to another facility. A transfer facility at a TSDF is any transportation-related area, such as a loading dock, parking area, or storage area. The TSDF may transfer materials from vehicles to its own facility or prepare rejected waste for transfer to another TSDF that can manage the waste.

Management Options for Hazardous Waste at Final Destination

Hazardous waste is ultimately sent to a treatment, storage, and disposal facility (TSDF). At the TSDF, a decision is made regarding how to manage the waste. It can be treated, stored, or disposed of, as follows:

- Waste may be treated in such a manner that the hazardous characteristics are removed or altered. Treatment can include such processes as incineration or oxidation. Treated waste may have viability for reuse in other manufacturing settings, or the treatment may reduce the volume of waste that must be managed.
- The facility will often temporarily store the material until such time as it is treated or disposed of. Waste may be stored in tanks, bulk containers, buildings, staging areas, or waste piles. Waste may be treated on site or moved to another facility for treatment or disposal.
- Waste that is disposed of is placed into specially designed landfills for permanent storage. The landfills undergo extensive permitting and regulation to prevent materials from leaching into the surrounding environment. A major focus of these preventions is on movement through groundwater and other surface waters.

Non-Disposal Strategies for Waste Materials

The Environmental Protection Agency (EPA) has established a **waste management hierarchy** that places disposal as the last resort. For wastes that cannot be eliminated or reduced, the other non-disposal options include recycling and reusing.

Recycling involves using an item designated as waste from one product as a **feedstock** for a different product. Examples of recycling include using petroleum processing wastes to make asphalt, and using glass scrap (termed "cullet") in formulations for new glass.

Reusing is when waste is reinserted into a process. Materials may be deemed as waste at the facility where they are generated but still have value to other industries. Now called "**secondary materials**," reusable materials include byproducts, spent materials, sludges, commercial chemical products, and scrap metal. An example of reuse is used solvents being repurposed as fuel for burners in other industrial processes.

Hazardous Materials Management Unit

A **hazardous materials management unit** is a plot of land where hazardous waste is placed, stored, or treated. Units include:

- Containers – portable devices that contain hazardous waste; includes the land on which such devices are located
- Tanks – stationary steel, plastic, fiberglass, or concrete vessels used to store or treat hazardous waste
- **Drip pads** – a basin surrounded by berms; used at wood preservation facilities
- **Containment buildings** – a self-supporting enclosed structure

- Incinerators – an enclosed combustion unit for thermally treating waste
- Boilers and furnaces – units that combust waste but use the energy produced for other purposes; includes kilns and halogen acid furnaces
- Landfills – excavated sites for nonliquid hazardous waste
- **Surface impoundments** – lined earthen depressions or excavations for liquid hazardous waste
- Waste piles – temporary storage areas for noncontainerized waste
- **Land treatment units** – areas where waste is applied to the soil and is treated using naturally occurring soil microbes and sunlight
- **Injection wells** – a location where liquid hazardous waste is injected belowground into porous soils.

Design Requirements for Hazardous Waste Landfills

A landfill is an engineered depression where solid waste is deposited. Modern landfills are subject to strict design, operation, and closure restrictions. Specialized landfills that are appropriately permitted can be used for hazardous waste disposal. To prevent chemicals from leaching into the soil and potentially into nearby groundwater, design requirements for a hazardous waste landfill include double liners, double leachate collection and removal systems, leak detection systems, precipitation run-on and runoff controls, wind dispersion controls, and construction quality assurance programs.

Post-Closure Requirements for Hazardous Waste Landfills

Hazardous waste landfills are permanent storage sites for solid hazardous waste. When the landfill has reached capacity, it must be properly closed and monitored over the long term. The intent of monitoring is to determine whether hazardous chemicals are escaping the landfill and contaminating the environment. To close the landfill, the operator must install and maintain the final **cover**. A leachate collection and removal system must run and be monitored until no more leachate is produced by the site. The leak detection system must remain in place, and groundwater must be monitored for 30 years after closure.

Hazardous Waste Management Hierarchy

To assist generators in determining how to manage hazardous waste, the Environmental Protection Agency (EPA) has developed a hazardous waste management hierarchy. The goals of any waste management program are to reduce the total amount of waste generated, preserve limited landfill space, and protect the environment during the management process. The hierarchy has four tiers ordered from most preferred to least preferred, as follows:

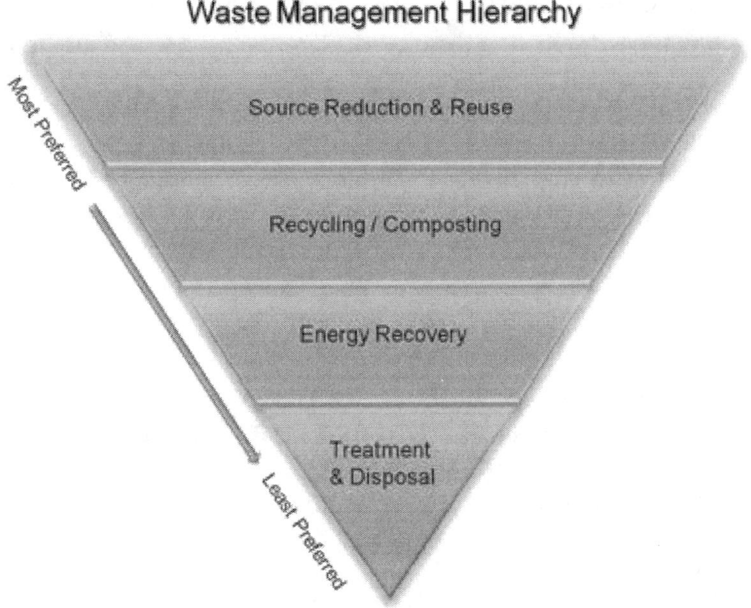

- **Source reduction** (most preferred) – By using nonhazardous or less hazardous materials at a facility, the volume of hazardous waste generated by that facility can be reduced or even eliminated.
- Recycle/Reuse – If a process generates a material that can either be reinserted into the original process or serve as a material for another process, company, or industry, then the material can be managed as a material of trade and not as waste.
- **Energy recovery** – Some wastes may have value as an energy source in other processes, as in the case of organic solvents being used as fuel for boilers or furnaces.
- Treatment or disposal (least preferred) – Treatment typically requires the use of other hazardous chemicals, which present their own hazards; however, the final product of treatment is typically nonhazardous. The last option is permanent storage of the material, typically in a permitted hazardous waste landfill.

Determining What Hazardous Waste Must Be Treated

The Environmental Protection Agency (EPA) has established a list of wastes that cannot be disposed of in a permitted landfill until they have been treated. Wastes that fall under this category are listed in the **Treatment Standards for Hazardous Waste** table. Wastes can be found in the table by determining the appropriate EPA waste code and determining if it is on the table. If a waste is in the table, a treatment method must be used to reduce the **regulated hazardous constituents** to a level that is below the listed concentration.

Determining Treatment Method for a Hazardous Waste

Prior to sending a hazardous waste to a disposal site, the sender must first determine if the waste must be treated and how it must be treated. The **treatment determination** is made by assigning an appropriate waste code to the material and determining if the code is listed on the Treatment Standards for Hazardous Waste table. If the waste code is on the table, the treatment technology will be listed in all caps in the last two columns, titled "Wastewater" and "Nonwastewater." The required treatment technology is listed in the **Treatment Standards Expressed as Specified Technologies** standard.

Selecting a Facility to Manage Hazardous Waste

The generator is responsible for selecting the appropriate facility to receive their hazardous waste. The generator must select a facility that is properly permitted not only to receive hazardous waste but also to receive the waste they are generating. Researching the facility using state databases can assist the generator in determining whether there have been any violations, civil penalties, or other issues at the facility. Additionally, the facility must have an Environmental Protection Agency (EPA) identification number to receive the waste. Finally, the facility should be able to provide evidence of appropriate insurance in the event of a release or of necessary remediation costs after closure.

Disposition of Waste

Managing Contaminated Soil Designated as Waste

Soil that has been contaminated with hazardous chemicals must be evaluated to determine if it falls under the Land Disposal Restriction (LDR) program. If the soil is profiled and found to contain a **listed waste** (K-, P-, or U-listed) or to exhibit a hazardous characteristic, is must be managed.

Soil must be treated to achieve one of two benchmarks—either the hazardous constituent is reduced by 90 percent of the concentration determined in the profile or the hazardous chemicals do not exceed 10 times the **universal treatment standard** found in 40 CFR 268.48.

Lab Pack and Land Disposal Restriction Program Treatment Requirements

A **lab pack** is a waste containerization option where multiple small chemical waste containers are placed in a larger container, referred to as an **overpack**. Each overpack may only contain chemicals with similar hazard characteristics. For example, 10 one-liter bottles of acetone waste can be placed in the same overpack. Additionally, waste hexane bottles and waste pentane bottles can be placed in the same overpack.

Per the Environmental Protection Agency (EPA) Land Disposal Restriction program, lab packs can be incinerated without restriction unless the profile's waste code is listed in Appendix IV of 40 CFR 268. After incineration, the residues must be treated for heavy metals (specifically arsenic, barium, cadmium, chromium, lead, selenium, and silver) prior to land disposal.

Debris

The Environmental Protection Agency (EPA) defines **debris** as any manufactured object, plant material, animal matter, or geologic material that is larger than a tennis ball. The term "debris" is often associated with demolition, renovation, or other construction projects. Debris under this definition either exhibits a hazardous characteristic or is contaminated with a listed waste. Under this definition, wood trim containing lead paint must be managed as LDR debris.

The EPA further subclassifies hazardous debris into the three following types:

- Mixtures of debris – combinations of different debris, such as glass and wood combined into a single container
- Mixtures of contaminants – a single debris type that has multiple regulated contaminants, such as wood trim painted with both lead paint and paint containing chromium
- Waste **PCBs** – debris contaminated with **polychlorinated biphenyls**

Treatment Requirements for Subcategories of Construction Debris Under LDR Program

The Environmental Protection Agency (EPA) broadly defines debris as commonly being associated with construction projects, such as demolition and renovation projects. The EPA has established specific treatment guidelines for the three subcategories of debris under the Land Disposal Restriction program. These guidelines are as follows:

- Mixture of debris – The waste must be treated to achieve the standards for each type of material present.
- Mixture of contaminants – The waste must be treated for each contaminant present.
- Waste PCBs – Specific treatment guidelines are listed in 40 CFR 268.45.

Alternative Treatment Technologies for Hazardous Debris Under the LDR Program

Hazardous debris must be treated for each identified hazardous component or characteristic. One of three treatment technologies can be used: extraction, destruction, or immobilization.

Extraction is the selective removal of a contaminant from the gross debris, essentially isolating the hazardous material from the rest of the waste material. After extraction, the debris can be sent to a landfill while the extracted material is managed as hazardous waste. Extraction can be physical (as in the case of abrasive blasting or grinding), chemical (including oxidation, or removal of the material using a solvent), or thermal (using high temperature to remove the contaminant or destroy the contaminant).

Destruction can be accomplished either by thermal means (incineration) or by chemical means. Chemical methods include oxidation (such as treatment with bleach) or reduction (including treatment with ferrous salts). After destruction, any residual materials must be evaluated for hazardous constituents. If no longer hazardous, they may be sent to a landfill.

Immobilization is a process where the hazardous component is encased so that it will not escape into the environment. Immobilization can include techniques such as sealing and microencapsulation. Immobilized materials must be managed as hazardous waste.

RCRA Disposition Confirmation and Documentation

Uniform Hazardous Waste Manifest

A generator is responsible for the fate of hazardous waste from "cradle to grave." Under this concept, it is the generator's responsibility to make sure that a waste gets to a proper management facility and is treated, stored, or destroyed appropriately. As most generators do not transport hazardous waste, a third-party contractor is typically hired to haul the waste. This contract relationship does not transfer the responsibility of the generator. Thus, the **manifest system** was developed to track the movement of hazardous waste and to demonstrate that it was managed properly.

The Uniform Hazardous Waste Manifest is an Environmental Protection Agency (EPA) and Department of Transportation (DOT) required document that is used to track hazardous waste from the generator to the final destination. The form contains a description of the waste, a record of how much was removed, where the waste was destined, and how much was received. The document is signed by all who handle the waste to demonstrate its progress to the treatment, storage, and disposal facility (TSDF).

Uniform Hazardous Waste Manifest Tracking Process

The Uniform Hazardous Waste Manifest is critical to the ability of generators to demonstrate compliance with hazardous waste management regulations.

The manifest is completed by the generator and details all the waste that is being shipped. The manifest records the waste codes, the number and sizes of containers, and that proper packaging was used to prevent incidents during transportation. Each manifest has a unique number that will always be associated with that waste shipment. The generator signs the manifest attesting that all waste was properly characterized and identified, that all waste was properly packaged, and that the shipping vehicle was appropriately marked. The generator is termed the "shipper" and retains a copy of the manifest as a record of what was shipped.

The transporter signs the manifest, acknowledging their receipt of the shipment to remove the waste from the generator's facility. Upon the shipment's arrival at the treatment, storage, and disposal facility (TSDF), the shipper retains a copy of the manifest to demonstrate what they transported to the TSDF and that no containers went missing along the way. The manifest is then given to the TSDF.

The TSDF verifies the waste containers received and signs the manifest. They keep a copy, and a signed copy is sent to the generator and, if required, to the state agency responsible for oversight. The generator must compare the manifest copy received from the TSDF to the copy of the manifest they retained upon shipment. These two copies must be retained for at least three years as proof that the waste was shipped and received. If there are any discrepancies between the two copies, the generator must file a notice with the state.

Managing a Release at a TSDF

The Resource Conservation and Recovery Act (RCRA) governs the management of hazardous waste at a treatment, storage, and disposal facility (TSDF). Under RCRA, any chemical spill or release requires an emergency response. Thus, release control activities, including preventing the spread of the release, stopping the release, and cleaning up after the release, are covered by the **Hazardous Waste Operations and Emergency Response (HAZWOPER)** standard. All employees must be trained to the level of response activities they will execute, which can vary from first responders preventing exposures to technicians cleaning up the spilled chemicals.

Air Emission Management

Air Emission Standards for TSDFs That Treat Waste by Combustion

If a treatment, storage, and disposal facility (TSDF) elects to treat waste by way of combustion, their operations are subject to the **Clean Air Act**. Combustion methods used for treating hazardous waste include cement kilns, incinerators, boilers, and hydrochloric acid furnaces. Thus, all Title V requirements, including implementing maximum achievable control technology (MACT) to control emissions, apply to the treatment facility.

Managing Air Emissions at TSDFs

The Resource Conservation and Recovery Act (RCRA) required the Environmental Protection Agency (EPA) to develop a set of standards to manage the air emissions that are produced by treatment, storage, and disposal facilities (TSDFs) that manage hazardous waste. To that end, the EPA promulgated the **RCRA organic air emissions standards**, which address the air emissions from TSDFs that manage organic solvent waste or materials contaminated with solvents. These facilities must monitor and control their air emissions to reduce the environmental impact of their operations. The RCRA organic air emissions standards include requirements for tanks, leaks in the treatment systems, and process vents.

Control Device for Organic Air Emissions

A **control device** for organic air emissions is an apparatus whose primary function is to inhibit organic vapors from hazardous waste storage or processing from escaping into the atmosphere. Emissions from hazardous waste can contain toxic materials or hazardous air pollutants. Associated hazards include exposure to employees, exposure to surrounding communities, and introducing a flammability hazard in the presence of ignition sources. Control devices include **enclosed combustion devices** (also known as "enclosed flares"), **vapor recovery systems**, or **flares**.

Water Emission Management

Groundwater Monitoring Requirements

Treatment, storage, and disposal facilities (TSDFs) may manage hazardous waste in a landfill, surface impoundment, or land treatment unit and may also have waste piles awaiting disposition. In these **waste management units**, the waste may come into contact with precipitation or surface waters. The water can then leach through the soil and enter surrounding groundwater, carrying hazardous chemicals with it. As contaminated groundwater can impact surrounding communities, protecting this resource is a priority for the Environmental Protection Agency (EPA). Thus, a **groundwater monitoring** system is required by the Resource Conservation and Recovery Act (RCRA) to detect potential pollution as soon as possible so that corrective actions can be implemented.

Phases of Groundwater Monitoring Program

A permitted treatment, storage, and disposal facility (TSDF) must implement and comply with a groundwater monitoring program if it meets the criteria established by the Environmental Protection Agency (EPA). A monitoring program is required for any facility that uses a soil-based storage or treatment process or one that manages waste piles. The groundwater monitoring program consists of three sequential phases—**detection monitoring**, **compliance monitoring**, and **corrective action**. A facility may move back and forth between phases as conditions and test results allow. Resource Conservation and Recovery Act (RCRA) standards establish the number of wells and the appropriate depth required to ensure reliable and actionable results are obtained through the monitoring program.

Groundwater Detection Monitoring

The first phase of a groundwater monitoring program is the detection monitoring. In this phase, the facility evaluates samples to determine if a release has occurred.

A groundwater monitoring system consists of a series of wells drilled down into the uppermost **aquifer**. The system must have at least two monitoring locations—one downstream from the facility and one upstream. The data collected from upstream wells is compared to that from downstream well to determine if there are any elevated levels of contaminants. The treatment, storage, and disposal facility's (TSDF) permit will designate the specific contaminants to be evaluated. At least four samples must be collected and analyzed from each well semiannually.

If there is a **statistically significant increase (SSI)** in a monitored contaminant, the TSDF must notify the Environmental Protection Agency (EPA) and must initiate a compliance monitoring program.

Compliance Groundwater Monitoring

As the second phase of a groundwater monitoring program, compliance monitoring is the evaluation of aquifers for components detected during detection monitoring. Once a statistically significant increase (SSI) in any pollutant listed on the permit is detected, the site must begin a compliance monitoring program. Under compliance monitoring, samples that are positive for contaminants must be compared to compliance standards as part of the **groundwater protection standard (GWPS)** that is established for the facility.

Under compliance monitoring, four samples are collected from each well and compared to the levels listed in the GWPS. The frequency of sampling is established by the regional authority but must be at least semiannually. If the levels detected exceed the compliance standards listed in the GWPS, then a corrective action must be taken.

Groundwater Protection Standard When a Pollutant Is Detected in Groundwater Near TSDF

The groundwater protection standard (GWPS) establishes an **action plan** for a treatment, storage, and disposal facility (TSDF) that detects a statistically significant level of contaminant in its downstream groundwater. The GWPS serves the following purposes:

- Lists the hazardous chemicals that must be tested for
- Establishes the maximum allowable concentration for those chemicals based on background levels collected from the upstream wells, Clean Water Act maximum contaminant levels, or other levels established by the regional authority.
- Describes where the compliance monitoring samples must be collected from
- Delineates the period of time during which compliance monitoring must occur.

Corrective Action

If a contaminant is found during detection monitoring and is determined to exceed allowable levels during compliance monitoring, the treatment, storage, and disposal facility (TSDF) must take corrective actions to reduce the contaminant levels in the groundwater by establishing and implementing a plan.

Any corrective action plan must be approved by the regional authority, who will also establish a timeframe for completion of the plan. A determination must be made as to whether a contaminant has migrated beyond the **compliance points** established by the groundwater protection standard (GWPS) and how this migration will be addressed. The corrective action must be continued until the contaminant levels established in the GWPS have not been exceeded for three years. If the levels drop below the thresholds, the facility will move from the corrective action phase back into the compliance monitoring phase. If levels continue to drop, the facility may eventually return to detection monitoring.

Treatment of Groundwater

Every **groundwater treatment** option is designed to reduce the level of the contaminant below established thresholds. Which technology is selected will depend on the physical and chemical properties of the contaminant as well as the volume of water to be treated. Groundwater can be treated in place or above ground. **Treatment-in-place** involves injecting or pumping the treatment option into the water table. **External treatment** typically involves pumping the water from the aquifer, treating it above ground, and then pumping the treated water back into the earth.

Low-boiling organic chemicals can be removed by **air sparging**. In this technique, air is pumped into the aquifer. The bubbles agitate the solution and facilitate the removal of the volatile and semi-volatile organic compounds. **Activated carbon** can be injected into the water to adsorb contaminants while chemical or biological additives in the carbon decompose the adsorbed compounds. This method is more widely applicable than sparging as more chemicals are attracted to carbon than are removed by agitation. A third option is **in situ thermal heating**, where volatile and semi-volatile chemicals are removed by raising the temperature of the water by any of a variety of techniques.

Record Keeping and Reporting

Spill/Release Reporting Requirements

Reporting Requirements for Hazardous Substance Release

Any facility that stores or uses a substance listed by the Environmental Protection Agency (EPA) as an **extremely hazardous substance (EHS)** must notify the **National Response Center** whenever their facility releases an amount of an EHS or a substance that is hazardous under the Comprehensive Environmental Response, Compensation, and Liability Act (CERCLA) that exceeds the **reportable quantity** within any 24-hour period. Once a release in excess of the reportable quantity is detected, the facility must immediately notify the National Response Center.

Types of Releases Exempt from Notification Requirements

Under certain circumstances, the release of an extremely hazardous substance (EHS) or a substance that is hazardous under the Comprehensive Environmental Response, Compensation, and Liability Act (CERCLA) does not require reporting to the National Response Center. Such releases include:

- Releases that only expose individuals within the boundary of the facility
- Releases of exempted pesticides
- Releases of radionuclides from natural sources
- Releases of less than 1,000 pounds of nitrogen oxide or nitrogen dioxide
- Emissions from animal waste

Sheen Rule for Oil Spills in Water

The Clean Water Act (CWA) uses the criteria of the **sheen rule** to determine whether an oil release into water requires reporting. Under the sheen rule, a spill must be reported in the following situations:

- The released oil produces a visible sheen (manifesting itself as a visible or multicolored patch floating on top of the water) or discoloration of the water.
- The release violates local water standards.
- Sludges or **emulsions** (visible petroleum) are deposited under the water or appear on the shoreline.

According to these criteria, reporting is not to be based on amount of product discharged.

Reporting Requirements for Oil Releases Under the CWA

The Clean Water Act (CWA) requires oil releases to be reported to the National Response Center (NRC). The report must be made immediately after the discharge is detected. The report of a discharge must include the following elements:

- Name, organization, and contact phone number of the reporting party
- Name and address of the party who discharged the material
- Date and time of the incident
- Location of the incident
- Source and cause of the discharge
- Type of material that was discharged into the water
- Quantity of material that was discharged

- Risk posed by the discharge to any local or downstream locations
- Any injuries that occurred as a result of the discharge
- Weather conditions at the location
- Any other information requested by the NRC

FILING WITH IMPLEMENTING AGENCIES FOR USTS

An **implementing agency** is a state agency that oversees **underground storage tank (UST)** regulations. UST standards identify five occasions when a report must be filed with the agency:

- When a UST is installed
- When ownership of a UST changes
- When a UST is to be used for a different product that requires notification per the implementing agency (e.g., when switching from pure gasoline to a 10 percent ethanol formulation)
- Whenever there is a suspected release from the UST, including follow-up plans to remediate the surrounding area
- When a UST is to be permanently closed

Record Keeping

EMERGENCY PLANNING AND COMMUNITY RIGHT TO KNOW ACT

ELEMENTS

The Environmental Protection Agency (EPA) is assigned responsibility for enforcing the **Emergency Planning and Community Right to Know Act (EPCRA)**. This act was created to help communities plan for chemical emergencies that could originate from companies in or around their area that store or handle toxic chemicals. The intent of the EPCRA is to increase community knowledge and access to information regarding chemicals at nearby facilities, including the uses of the chemicals and the provisions for managing potential releases. EPCRA addresses four main elements—planning, notification, information, and reporting, as follows:

- Planning – Facilities that store large amounts of toxic or hazardous chemicals are required to cooperate with local agencies in preparing **emergency release response plans**.
- Notification – Facilities must immediately report any release of hazardous substances that exceed a designated reportable quantity (RQ).
- Information – In order to inform the community, facilities must provide local response agencies with the safety data sheets (SDSs) of the materials on site as well as an inventory delineating those chemicals.
- Reporting – Facilities must annually submit a toxic release inventory—a report of the releases of specified chemicals that exceed certain thresholds.

NOTIFICATION REQUIREMENTS FOR FACILITIES

Facilities that maintain listed substances above their threshold planning quantity must provide information to their **local emergency planning committee (LEPC)**, the **state emergency response commission (SERC)**, and the local fire department, as appropriate.

For all listed materials considered hazardous under the Comprehensive Environmental Response, Compensation, and Liability Act (CERCLA), and for all substances considered extremely hazardous materials under the Emergency Planning and Community Right to Know Act (EPCRA), facilities must provide an inventory of each chemical and the associated safety data sheets (SDS) within three months of beginning operations.

Inventory Requirements

Facilities that are subject to the Emergency Planning and Community Right to Know Act (EPCRA) based on the presence of hazardous materials and extremely hazardous substances on site must annually update the inventory with the local emergency planning committee (LEPC), the state emergency response commission (SERC), and the local fire department. The inventory applies to all EPCRA extremely hazardous substances and CERCLA hazardous materials.

The inventory must contain site-identifying information, such as the business name and address, as well as contact information. For each listed substance, the inventory must show:

- The chemical or common name as found on the SDS
- The estimated **maximum daily amount** at any time for the past 12 months, as well as an average daily amount
- A description of storage conditions at the facility for the substance
- Where the chemical is located on the premises
- Whether the location of the material should be withheld from the public

Toxic Substances Control Act

Intent

The **Toxic Substances Control Act (TSCA)** gives the Environmental Protection Agency (EPA) the authority to regulate chemical substances that are not specifically regulated under other standards or policies. Examples of substances that did not meet the criteria of other regulations included asbestos, formaldehyde, and polychlorinated biphenyls (PCBs). The intent of TSCA is to determine if a substance presents a high risk to people or the environment and, if so, to establish controls for the substance.

TSCA requires that manufacturers or processors of chemical substances test these substances, as required by the act, to determine if they pose a risk to health or the environment. Test results must be submitted to the EPA to determine whether the substance must be regulated by TSCA or can be exempted from it.

PMN

The Toxic Substances Control Act (TSCA) requires that, before a new chemical or substance is manufactured, the manufacturing facility file a **premanufacture notice (PMN)** with the Environmental Protection Agency (EPA). The PMN allows the EPA to estimate the health and environmental risk the substance may pose as it is used or transported for commerce. The PMN must include the following information:

- Applicant's name
- Chemical substance's identity (name or other identifier)
- Production volume
- Uses
- Available exposure data
- Available environmental fate data

Actual test data need not accompany a PMN, but an applicant should provide all available information with the application. Required testing can occur later in the process.

SIGNIFICANT NEW USE RULE

The **significant new use rule (SNUR)** is an Environmental Protection Agency (EPA) notification process for using substances in a new manner that may create concern. The EPA applies the new use criteria to a chemical substance when, due to the new manner of use or production, one of the following is true: the volume well exceeds volumes in prior processes; the mode of exposure to humans or the environment changes; exposure to humans or the environment becomes greater; or the method of production, processing, or disposal is drastically altered.

If the EPA determines that the substance is subject to the SNUR, the facility must provide the EPA a **significant new use notice (SNUN)** no less than 90 days before manufacturing or importing can begin. Once the EPA receives the SNUN, they evaluate the risks and determine what, if any, additional regulations apply to the new use.

TESTING CATEGORIES FOR NEW MATERIALS

New materials not already listed in the Toxic Substances Control Act (TSCA), managed by the Environmental Protection Agency (EPA), must undergo testing to evaluate the risk they pose to workers and the environment. Manufacturers must first determine if a substance is exempted under TSCA. If not exempted, new substances must be evaluated for three categories:

- **Chemical fate** – chemical and physical properties, including how soluble the material is in both water and soil, how it moves through an environment, its susceptibility to solar radiation, and whether the chemistry of the environment, such as exposure to water or microbes, will create other toxic substances
- Environmental effects – including toxicity to aquatic animals and algae
- Health effects – toxicity for both acute and chronic exposures, including any organ-specific toxicity, genetic toxicity, and neurotoxicity

Test results for these categories are uploaded into the EPA system, where the results await review and approval.

RECORD RETENTION REQUIREMENTS FOR USTS

Owners and operators of **underground storage tanks (UST)** must have a **leak detection system** installed. The intent of the system is to detect any potential subterranean migration of chemicals from the tank into nearby groundwater. Thus, the following system **records** must be kept in the event an agency inspector comes on site:

- **Proof of performance** claims provided by the manufacturer or installer. These must be kept for at least five (5) years
- **Calibration and maintenance schedules** as provided by the manufacturer must be kept for five (5) years after installation
- **Sampling, testing, and monitoring** results of the leak detection system for the past year
- All calibration, maintenance, and repair records for the detection system for one (1) year from the service date.

Underground storage tanks (USTs) present a high risk of leaching material into nearby groundwater or contaminating the soil in the environment, resulting in contaminants spreading into the surrounding community. Thus, these units require extensive recordkeeping, including the following:

- The previous three 60-day rectifier inspections
- The previous two **corrosion protection system tests**, which occur every three years; in cases where no corrosion protection system is in use for metal pipes and the tank, a record of the corrosion expert's analysis of the corrosion potential kept for the life of the UST
- Any upgrades or repairs until the system is closed
- Permanent closure site assessment records must be kept for three years after the UST is closed
- Documents certifying the business's financial responsibility in the event a leak is detected
- For modified regulated substances as identified by the implementing agency, compatibility compliance records
- Three previous years of **spill bucket** testing, **sump** testing, and **overfill inspections**; in cases where no spill buckets or sumps are in use, records of **double-wall construction** as well as periodic inspection of double-walls as long as no testing is conducted
- One previous year of records
- Operator training records

Compliance Monitoring

Numerous programs enforced by the Environmental Protection Agency (EPA) require that any company that produces, stores, uses, or discharges hazardous chemicals adhere to the applicable regulations. Not having enough inspectors for every regulated facility **walk-through inspection**, the EPA relies on compliance monitoring as the primary tool for making sure that facilities are following laws.

Monitoring has multiple elements, including on-site inspections, recordkeeping, mandatory report submissions, and public complaints or tips. All of these tools are used to determine if a facility is complying with the regulations that pertain to their operations. Any evidence of a potential failure could result in an on-site inspection.

Stack Test

A **stack test**, also referred to as a "**performance test**" or "**source test**," is a method the Environmental Protection Agency (EPA) uses to determine if a facility is adhering to their emission requirements under the Clean Air Act (CAA). It is used when no other method (such as monitoring emissions remotely) can be used to determine adherence to emission requirements. The test is a **direct measurement** of the emissions from a point source of emissions and measures the amount of specific pollutants escaping into the environment. Samples are collected from ports in the stack, which are then analyzed in the field or in a laboratory.

Recordkeeping Requirements for Stationary Sources Under the CAA

To verify that a facility is remaining under its emission thresholds for air pollutants, the Clean Air Act (CAA) requires certain facilities to retain records and make reports to the Environmental Protection Agency (EPA).

The facility must keep records of any startup, shutdown, malfunction, or other interruption that could affect either the monitoring systems or the control devices. If a continuous monitoring device is required by permit, the facility must submit a **monitoring system report**, including any excess emissions, every six months to the regulating agency.

All emissions measurements and monitoring device performance records must be kept by the facility for at least two years. Device performance records must include performance evaluations, calibration checks, adjustments, and maintenance. If a facility uses a **continuous emissions monitoring system (CEMS)**, the retained data must be of the most recent three sub-hourly measurement averages.

Discharge Monitoring Report – Quality Assurance Program

Facilities that require a major permit under the **National Pollutant Discharge Elimination System (NPDES)** as well as selected minor permit holders must participate in the **Discharge Monitoring Report - Quality Assurance Program**. This program uses annual **proficiency test samples** to evaluate the laboratories used by permit holders for self-monitoring. The permit holder must submit the results of these test samples only for those analytes that are listed on the facility's permit. Through this program, the Environmental Protection Agency (EPA) ensures that the laboratories used to monitor discharges are producing reliable results.

Reports Required Under the Clean Water Act

Holders of permits under the National Pollutant Discharge Elimination System (NPDES) must submit three types of reports:

- **Discharge Monitoring Reports (DMR)** - results of self-monitoring tests of wastewater discharges to demonstrate compliance with the permit under which the facility is operating. Depending on the permit, these reports may be due to the permit-administering agency on a monthly, quarterly, semiannual, or annual basis.
- **Notice of Intent (NOI)** to discharge - a form submitted by a marine vessel indicating that they will be discharging regulated pollutants under the Vessel General Permit program of the Environmental Protection Agency (EPA)
- **Other specified program reports** - other reports that may be required by the operating permit

Recordkeeping Requirements Under the HMTA

The **Hazardous Material Transportation Act (HMTA)** requires that employers retain records of employee training for the current year and the three previous years. Training records must be kept for each employee for that period and for 90 days after an employee leaves that employer. The record must include the following:

- The employee's name
- The date of training
- A description of the training or a copy of the training materials
- The name and address of the person who provided the training
- Certification that the training was successfully completed and that a test was passed as required.

Recordkeeping Requirements Under the RCRA

As the primary regulation for monitoring hazardous waste, the Resource Conservation and Recovery Act (RCRA) requires hazardous waste generators to produce and retain various records.

What exact records must be kept is determined by the type and volume of hazardous waste generated by the facility. Records that may need to be kept include the following:

- **Waste analysis plans** must be kept for three years after the last date waste was treated on site for generators who treat waste on site without a permit to meet the Land Disposal Restriction requirements.
- Land Disposal Restriction paperwork, including the notification of certification and supporting documentation, must be retained for three years from the date the waste was shipped.
- Annual training records must be kept for the duration of an employee's time with the facility plus three years, for large quantity generators.
- Hazardous waste manifests must be kept for three years.
- **Exception reports**, records of manifests that were not received back from a destination facility, must be retained for three years.
- **Hazardous waste determination** reports, which are records of how the generator classified their waste, must be kept for three years.

Training Personnel

Training Required for Hazardous Material Spill Response Team

The Occupational Safety and Health Administration (OSHA) identifies five different levels of employee training for chemical spill response: first responder awareness, first responder operations, hazardous materials technician, hazardous materials specialist, and on-site commander.

A **first responder awareness** employee is one who will respond to a spill, keep others out of the area, and initiate a response by contacting the appropriate personnel. They will not be involved in containing or cleaning up the release. These individuals must understand the risk hazardous substances present, how to recognize a spill or release, what to do when a spill is identified, and who needs to be contacted.

A **first responder operations** employee is one who will respond to a release to prevent the spill from getting worse and work to protect the environment and other people in the area of the spill. They respond defensively but do not attempt to stop the release. In addition to being trained on the material for the awareness level, these individuals must be trained on how to select and wear protective equipment, how to contain chemical releases, and basic decontamination procedures.

Hazardous materials technicians will respond to a release with the intent of stopping the release at the source. They must have at least the same level of knowledge as a first responder operations employee. They must also be trained on field identification techniques for unknown chemicals, understand the **Incident Command System**, be able to select and properly use specialized protective equipment, and have an understanding of basic toxicology and chemical terminology.

Hazardous materials specialists are similar to hazardous materials technicians, but their knowledge base is focused on specific substances.

The **on-site commander** must be trained to the first responder awareness level but must also have an understanding of the Incident Command System, the employer's **emergency response plan**, local emergency response plans, regional and federal response capabilities, and the hazards associated with employees working in chemical protective equipment.

The employer determines what level of response their employees will conduct when a spill is detected and arrange for additional support if the need exceeds their capabilities.

Training Requirements for Asbestos Abatement Under the Toxic Substances Control Act

Under the **Asbestos Model Accreditation Program (MAP)**, employees involved in asbestos inspections or response actions at schools or other public buildings must be trained. MAP establishes five levels of training:

- Worker – for those who will abate identified asbestos materials or conduct maintenance that may disturb friable asbestos
- **Contractor/supervisor** – for those who will supervise certified MAP workers
- **Inspector** – for individuals who will inspect schools or other public buildings to identify potential asbestos-containing materials

- **Management planner** – for employees who will prepare asbestos management plans for public buildings; must be a certified inspector prior to being certified as a management planner
- **Project designer** – certification for employees who will design activities for asbestos-related activities.

Employees must undergo an initial training approved by the applicable state agency as well as annual refreshers.

Asbestos Awareness Training Required Under OSHA

Due to its hazards, asbestos is one of the materials that the Occupational Safety and Health Administration (OSHA) has devoted an individual standard to. Under 29 CFR 1910.1001, OSHA delineates exposure limits and hazard mitigation requirements for exposure to asbestos. In this standard, OSHA outlines training requirements for employees who may be exposed to airborne asbestos at or above the permissible exposure limit. Training must address the following:

- Asbestos-related health effects
- The connection between smoking, asbestos, and lung cancer
- What specific operations at the facility may result in an exposure to asbestos-containing materials, including where those materials are located
- Controls to reduce or eliminate asbestos fiber exposure
- Proper procedures to reduce exposure when working with or near asbestos
- The employer's asbestos medical surveillance program
- The content of the OSHA asbestos standard
- Local smoking cessation programs
- Required signage used to identify locations of asbestos at the facility

Training Requirements for Lead Abatement

Lead presents a unique hazard that is emphasized by both the Occupational Safety and Health Administration (OSHA) and the Environmental Protection Agency (EPA) as a substance of concern. Lead abatement activities are specifically designed to permanently eliminate the hazard of lead-based paints. Individuals and firms who renovate, repair, and paint (RRP) houses, pre-schools, and childcare facilities built before 1978 that have lead-based paint must be certified. There are certifications in two disciplines:

- **Renovator** – performs visual inspections to determine that lead-containing dusts have been removed after work has been completed; cleans up spaces where lead-containing dusts have been removed
- **Dust sampling technician** – performs post-project air sampling to verify that the environment is below the established threshold for lead dust

Training Requirements for Operators of HMIWIs

A **hospital, medical, and infectious waste incinerator (HMIWI)** is not allowed to burn waste unless a certified operator is on site. Operators are certified by state agencies and must complete at least 24 hours of training that covers the following:

- Emissions from HMIWI facilities and their environmental impact
- Basic combustion principles
- Proper startup, operation, and shutdown of the incinerator
- Combustion controls and monitoring systems

- Operation of the air pollution control equipment installed at the facility
- Monitoring system calibration processes
- Malfunction correction and underlying causes
- Characteristics and how to manage **bottom ash** and **fly ash**
- Applicable regulations
- Safety procedures
- System pre-startup inspections
- Recordkeeping requirements

Classes of Certifications for UST Operators

Underground storage tank (UST) operators, those who have a UST at their facility, must undergo operator training to satisfy Environmental Protection Agency (EPA) requirements. There are three classes of operators:

- **Class A** – operators who will be responsible for compliance and are determining whether the appropriate individuals are fulfilling the operation, recordkeeping, and maintenance requirements for the UST on site
- **Class B** – individuals who will be directly responsible for the operation, maintenance, and recordkeeping of the UST
- **Class C** – trained by either a Class A or a Class B operator, individuals who will respond to alarms or emergency releases of the contents of the UST and must be trained in the appropriate actions to take in such situations

Class A and Class B operators must receive training within 30 days of assuming duties while Class C operators must be trained before assuming their duties.

Training Topics Required for Class A Operators of USTs

Class A underground storage tank (UST) operators are responsible for the overall compliance monitoring of the UST. Thus, they must receive training in the following topics:

- Spill and overfill prevention
- Detecting releases of tank contents
- The concepts of corrosion protection
- Emergency responses to releases
- Compatibility considerations between the stored product and the tank itself
- Financial responsibility and requirements of the business that operates the UST
- The process of registering the UST and notifying the state agency of any changes
- The process and requirements for both temporary and permanent closures of the UST
- The inspection, testing, reporting, and recordkeeping requirements for all phases of the lifecycle of a UST
- The environmental impact of any release from the UST and the associated regulations, including required notifications
- Training requirements for Class B and Class C operators, whose activities they will likely direct

Hazmat Employer

The Department of Transportation (DOT) requires that hazmat employees be trained properly by their employer. DOT uses the term "**hazmat employer**" to refer to any business that uses one or more employees to perform the following services:

- Transport hazardous materials, including waste, as part of a commercial venture
- Prepare or package hazardous materials for shipment, including waste
- Sell or manufacture packaging designed for hazardous materials shipment (a broadly defined set of services that includes reconditioning, fabricating, inspecting, and marking hazardous materials packaging)

Hazmat employers must train hazmat employees and test them on their knowledge. The employer must also certify the training and retain records of the training for the required period, typically no less than three years.

Hazmat Employee

A **hazmat employee**, per the US Department of Transportation (DOT), either works for a hazmat employer or is self-employed. These employees must undergo proper training on handling and packaging hazardous materials. Individuals qualify as hazmat employees if their work involves performing any of the following tasks:

- Driving or operating a vehicle that transports hazardous materials, including waste
- Loading, unloading, or otherwise handling hazardous materials
- Making, manipulating, reconditioning, or otherwise preparing for use any packaging used for hazardous materials shipments
- Packaging hazardous materials for shipment
- Supervising or otherwise being responsible for the safe shipment of hazardous materials

General DOT Hazmat Training Requirements for Hazmat Employees

Training hazmat employees is a requirement for all hazmat employers. Employees must be trained on the following topics:

- General awareness and familiarization with hazardous materials, including hazard classes, required markings and labeling, modes of chemical exposure, protective measures to prevent exposure, and spill or emergency response measures
- Function-specific training for the job the employee will perform, including necessary precautions and control measures
- Chemical and personal safety
- Shipment security awareness and how to prevent unauthorized diversion of hazardous materials
- For operations that require a security plan based on the volume or type of substances, in-depth security measures to prevent unauthorized access to materials
- Driver training for those who will operate the vehicles

Initial Training and Refresher Training Frequency for DOT Hazmat Training

Initial training for hazmat employees must occur within 90 days of assignment to a job that involves hazardous materials handling or shipping. This requirement implies that an employee may perform tasks related to or involving hazardous material prior to being trained but can only do so if supervised by a properly trained individual. Refresher training is required every three years after the initial training.

Training Requirements for Employees Who Sign Hazardous Waste Manifests

Generators of hazardous waste are responsible for preparing both the materials for shipment as well as the shipping papers. The Uniform Hazardous Waste Manifest (EPA Form 8700-22), the tracking document for hazardous waste shipments, contains a certification statement that is signed by the waste generator. The statement declares that the items described on the manifest are described using their proper shipping names and are properly classified and packaged based on the hazards they present. Additionally, the signatory certifies that the packages are properly marked and labeled for transport, including proper placarding of the transport vehicle. Thus, any employee who signs the Uniform Hazardous Waste Manifest must be trained in these areas, many of which are also requirements in DOT hazmat training.

Hazardous Material Competency Levels

Hazardous Materials Competency Levels Per the NFPA

The National Fire Prevention Association (NFPA) has developed Standard 472 to identify competencies for individuals who respond to hazardous materials incidents. The standard, titled "Standard for Competence of Responders to Hazardous Materials/Weapons of Mass Destruction Incidents," is designed to increase the safety of responders by outlining minimum knowledge for designated levels. These levels include:

- Awareness
- Operations
- Technicians
- Incident Commanders
- HazMat Officers
- Safety Officers
- Specialists

NFPA Standard 472 has been adopted by the Department of Homeland Security as the foundation for training programs for those who respond to weapons of mass destruction (WMD) incidents.

Competencies of Individuals Trained to the HazMat Awareness Level

An employee trained to the **Awareness** level is one who may encounter a hazardous materials emergency and will act in a defensive manner. Individuals trained to this level may include first responders and employees who work with or near processes involving hazardous materials.

The competencies for an Awareness level individual include the following:

- Recognizing the presence of hazardous materials by way of labels, placards, and warnings as well as understanding the various hazard classes
- Identifying hazardous materials using safety data sheets, inventories, or other information available at the facility
- Collecting information on the hazards presented by materials, including the use of the Emergency Response Guidebook
- Implementing an emergency response by understanding how to isolate the area to protect themselves and others and how to properly notify individuals with a higher level of training

Hazardous Materials Operations Level Responders

Operations level hazardous materials employees are those who will respond to a chemical release in an offensive manner. The goal of the Operations level is to protect persons, property, and the environment from the impacts of the chemical. Competencies for the Operations level include the following:

- All competencies for the Awareness level.
- Analyzing the incident, which includes surveying the incident to identify the materials and containers involved, collecting information from available sources on the hazards and response activities for the materials involved, predicting the behavior of the material and its container under the conditions of the incident, and estimating the potential harm based on chemical conditions, environmental conditions, and the location, and by monitoring results.
- Planning the response, which involves describing the response objectives, identifying action options to achieve the objectives, selecting proper personal protective equipment (PPE), and identifying required decontamination procedures.
- Implementing the response activities, including establishing site control to prevent the spread of the chemical, preserving evidence to allow for post-incident evaluation, initiating the Incident Command System and all associated elements, and properly using PPE.
- Evaluating progress of the response by way of assessing the effectiveness of control actions and how to communicate progress through the chain of command.

Role and Competencies for Hazardous Materials Safety Officers During Chemical Release Responses

A hazardous materials **Safety Officer** is responsible for ensuring all site activities are executed in a safe manner during a chemical incident response. In addition to understanding all the competencies the other levels, the Safety Officer must have the following competencies:

- Analyzing the incident by implementing a risk-based evaluation of all data collected at the site to maximize safety during the response
- Assisting in the development of the response plan by identifying the required safety precautions, recommending control measures for employee safety, assisting in the development of the **site safety plan** portion of the Incident Action Plan, acting as a consultant to other levels, reviewing personal protective equipment recommendations, reviewing decontamination procedures, ensuring that emergency medical services are available and appropriate, reviewing site control procedures, reviewing implementation of **control zones**, and making sure that all persons involved in a response are appropriately trained
- Implementing safety procedures including monitoring response personnel, conducting safety briefings, enforcing site control, and implementing **exposure monitoring**
- Evaluating progress during the response for any deviations from the safety plan and implementing any corrective actions
- Terminating their portion of the response, including making the necessary reports, conducting a safety debrief, and assisting in the post-incident critique

Agencies to Include in Facility's Chemical Release Drills or Planning

Pre-emergency planning is crucial in reducing the impact of accidental releases of hazardous material on people, the environment, and the company. Some businesses may elect to have in-house emergency response services while others may either contract out the service or rely on local first responder agencies. The degree of interaction and planning with external agencies will be driven by the volume and types of materials stored on site as well as the resources available to the organization.

Businesses that use extremely hazardous substances are required to interact with local fire agencies as well as local or regional governmental emergency response teams. Thus, drills should include local fire agencies and regional emergency response groups to work through challenges, improve communication, build relationships, understand limitations, and give external agencies an opportunity to come on site to familiarize themselves with the actual layout of the facility. Emergency preparedness drills can also include the relevant environmental agencies, such as regional air quality control boards, water quality agencies, and local environmental health agencies. Including these groups in pre-emergency planning will facilitate an effective response to a spill or release.

Evaluating Training Adequacy

Assessing an Employee's Competency

Competency (defined as possessing sufficient knowledge or skill) should be assessed to determine whether an employee requires supplemental training or resources to work safely. The following four methods can be used to assess competency:

- **Tests** – The most common method is to give an employee a test to evaluate their knowledge of the topic. This method is inexpensive and easy to execute. The shortcoming of testing is that it only evaluates knowledge, not ability.
- **Self-assessment** – The employee provides feedback on their own abilities. The benefit of a self-assessment lies in the fact that the employee can identify areas where they feel they need to improve. This method can have the drawback of employees who do not want to appear substandard making unrealistic assessments of their shortcomings.
- **Feedback** – The supervisor or coworkers provide feedback on the abilities of the employee. Feedback has the advantage of being objective and is based on past performance. This method suffers from the potential of bias as personal feelings can impact the truthfulness of the assessment.
- **Skills tests** – The employee demonstrates their abilities in a controlled environment. This method is beneficial in that the assessment demonstrates what the employee can do, is not biased against those who struggle with written tests, and can test the ability of an employee to adapt to situations. However, this method can be expensive if a test laboratory must be constructed or if the observation slows the production line.

Competency-Based Safety Training

Competency-based training (CBT) is a method of safety training that requires employees to demonstrate their acquisition of the knowledge and skills conveyed during training. Instead of only verifying that an individual has received the information (typically evaluated using a written test), this method relies on performance-based assessments that allow the employee to demonstrate their understanding and application of the knowledge. For example, instead of having an employee complete a written exam on the steps needed to check a respirator prior to use, the evaluator would give the employee a respirator and observe them conducting the checks while donning the respirator.

Determining Training Course Duration

Certain regulations and standards establish required training for employees, supervisors, and others to ensure that specific material is covered. Environmental Protection Agency (EPA),

Department of Transportation (DOT), and Occupational Safety and Health Administration (OSHA) standards will typically outline the required elements of a training program that would qualify employees to execute job tasks under a particular standard. In some instances, the regulation or standard does not explicitly state a timeframe or duration for training. For example, for training on underground storage tanks (USTs), EPA regulations only outline topics to be covered, not how long training should take. However, under the OSHA Hazardous Waste Operations and Emergency Response (HAZWOPER) standard, different certifications have different time requirements (eight hours for first responders, 24 hours for technicians). Thus, it is critical to refer to the relevant standards to ensure any duration requirements for training programs are met.

Non-Classroom Methods for Health and Safety Training

The Occupational Safety and Health Administration (OSHA) places high value on training. Recently, OSHA has shifted toward the concept of effective training, meaning that employees must not only be presented the information but must achieve an understanding that allows them to apply the concepts to work in a safe manner. OSHA has identified three methods of effective training that occur outside of the traditional classroom setting, as follows:

- **Peer-to-peer training**, where an experienced employee provides instruction and direction on how to execute tasks.
- **On-the-job training**, where an employee learns by doing, supervised by a qualified and properly trained supervisor or other superior.
- **Worksite demonstrations**, where training occurs outside of the classroom and in the "natural" environment of the task or job.

Response and Recovery

National Response Center Spill Reporting

National Response Center

The **National Response Center (NRC)** is a federal reporting system for any oil, chemical, radiological, biological, or etiological (disease-causing) discharge in the United States or its territories. The NRC is staffed 24 hours a day by the US Coast Guard as they also process reports of suspicious maritime activities. Any report to the NRC will activate the **National Contingency Plan** for a response. The NRC will record the size and nature of the release, the facility involved, and the party responsible for the release and will forward that information to the on-scene coordinator.

National Response System

The **National Response System (NRS)** is a federal mechanism that is activated to respond to oil or chemical releases into the environment. Response teams are composed of federal, state, local, tribal, industrial, and organizational representatives to provide a broad array of expertise and experience. The intent of the NRS is to provide **subject matter experts** who can ensure that timely and efficient cleanups are executed to minimize the threats to and impacts on the environment. They are deployed whenever a release requires resources that are beyond that of local and state responders.

The **National Response System (NRS)** is a mechanism that provides assistance to state and local responders when oil or chemical releases exceed their capabilities, either because of the scope of the release or because of the hazard presented by the material.

The NRS is activated when the entity responsible for a release contacts the **National Response Center (NRC).** After information is collected by the NRC, the NRC will contact a designated **on-scene commander** assigned to the region where the release occurred. The NRC will also contact local and state response personnel. The on-scene commander will coordinate with the responding agencies and the responsible party to determine whether the deployed resources are sufficient for management of the release. Once an assessment is made regarding the available capabilities, the commander will determine whether federal resources are necessary and, if so, deploy those resources.

Providing Information for Release of Hazardous Substance

Facilities must notify the **National Response Center (NRC)** in the event of a qualifying release. The facility must immediately provide the following information:

- Chemical or substance **name**
- Whether the substance is an extremely hazardous substance (EHS)
- Estimated release amount
- Time and duration of the release
- Whether the release was into air, soil, or water
- Known or anticipated acute and chronic health effects of the released substance and any recommended medical attention for exposed individuals
- Proper precautions to take, including recommended evacuations
- Name and phone number of a contact at the reporting facility

Additionally, the facility must follow up with a **written emergency notification** "as soon as practicable after the release" to the local or state emergency response coordinator. This notice must include any updates to the information in the initial notification as well as the following information:

- Actions taken to respond and keep the release from spreading.
- Any known health effects associated with the release.
- Any recommended medical treatment for exposed individuals.

Spill Response Plans

Emergency Action Plan

An unanticipated chemical release meets the Occupational Safety and Health Administration (OSHA) criteria for an emergency—an unplanned event that interrupts business operations and threatens employees, the public, or the environment. Thus, such releases should be anticipated and therefore included in the organization's emergency planning, forming an **emergency action plan (EAP)**. An EAP is a requirement for businesses that employ more than 10 people and must have the following elements:

- How an emergency is reported to the organization and to other employees, which should include an alarm system
- Procedures to properly evacuate employees from the facility, which must receive training on
- Who must remain behind during an evacuation to shut down critical procedures and equipment safely before evacuating themselves
- How the organization will make sure all employees and visitors have been evacuated
- Procedures for employees, if any, assigned to rescue and medical duties
- Who the employees can contact for additional information on the EAP

Emergency Action Plan vs. Emergency Response Plan

Planning for emergencies is critical for any business to prevent injuries, reduce losses, and resume operations as soon as possible. During an emergency is not the appropriate time to figure out what to do and who is responsible to do what. There are two types of plans typically required by regulatory agencies—an emergency action plan (EAP) and an **emergency response plan (ERP)**.

An EAP is typically defensive in nature; it describes how an employer will evacuate, where people will meet, how they will communicate with responding agencies, and how they will account for everyone. Additionally, an EAP can be applied to a variety of emergencies, including medical emergencies, active shooters, fires, earthquakes, and floods.

An ERP is used when an employer will take action to address the emergency. Whether it is for a hazardous material spill or a fire, an ERP delineates specific response elements for a particular type of emergency. The ERP will designate responders, outline their training, describe alarm systems, explain the equipment required for a response, outline how the team will integrate with external agencies (e.g., the fire department), and include a provision to review any responses for future improvement.

Release Response Steps

The response to a chemical release or spill is designed to reduce the impact on personnel and the environment, stop the release, and prevent the release from spreading. Thus, any spill should be addressed in the following steps:

- Step 1: Notification. Employees in the immediate area must be notified of the release or spill to reduce the risk of exposure. For larger releases that can impact nearby communities, larger-scale notifications may be necessary. Additionally, all relevant emergency response agencies and local emergency groups may require notification, depending on the scope and nature of the release.
- Step 2: Control. All attempts should be made to halt the release that can be made safely by properly equipped and trained personnel. By controlling the spill, personnel can ensure that the impact on the surrounding individuals and environment is as low as possible in the circumstances.
- Step 3: Contain. All actions should be taken to keep the release isolated to as small an area as possible. This may involve covering drains or using absorbent materials or berms to keep the material from exiting the immediate location.
- Step 4: Clean. After the release has been stopped and the spread has been contained, the cleanup can begin. All contaminated materials must be removed and managed as hazardous waste. Additionally, surfaces or areas may need to be thoroughly cleaned prior to restarting operations.

Containing and Cleaning Up Oil Spills

There are numerous methods that can be used to contain and clean oil spills on bodies of water. These methods can be divided into three classes of techniques:

- **Mechanical containment** or recovery – Mechanical means are designed to capture and store spilled oil so it can be disposed of properly. This technique is the most common technique for any oil release on water. It includes the use of booms, barriers, skimmers, and sorbent materials.
- Chemical and biological methods – These methods are designed to stop the spread or assist in the recovery of habitats affected by an oil spill. Chemical methods include gelling agents (which cause the liquid oil to form solid particles that can be removed from the water) or dispersing agents (which break the slick into smaller droplets to reduce the impact of the spill). Biological methods include deploying microorganisms that increase the breakdown rate of the oil in the environment.
- Physical methods – Typically applied to shoreline cleanup, physical methods remove the bulk of the material to allow the natural processes to work on whatever residue is left behind. Physical methods include wiping, pressure washing, and raking.

Facility Response Plan for Sites That Store and Use Oil

Businesses that are classified under the Oil Pollution Act as a **substantial harm facility** are those in areas where an oil discharge would substantially harm the environment. Facilities designated as such are required to have a **facility response plan (FRP)**. Typically, substantial harm facilities are those that move 42,000 gallons or more of oil over water or that are land-based and have a total capacity exceeding 1,000,000 gallons.

FRPs must be submitted to the Environmental Protection Agency (EPA) to plan for worst-case-scenario releases from the facility. An FRP ensures that the facility is prepared, in terms of equipment and trained personnel, to effectively respond to a release in a manner that reduces the impact and severity of the spill. The FRP also includes provisions for identifying risks of discharge in an effort to preemptively address them to reduce the chance of discharge. Finally, the FRP provides assisting agencies information on the scope of the operation at the facility as well as the organization's response capabilities and likely assistance needs.

Required Elements

Sites that store large quantities of oil near bodies of water must prepare a facility response plan (FRP). The FRP is an extensive plan that must have the following elements:

- An emergency action plan (EAP)
- Facility information, such as owner, operator, and location
- Emergency measures, such as personnel and equipment, even those that are by contract
- Risk assessment of potential discharge locations
- Assessment of small, medium, and worst-case-scenario spills as well as planned response actions for each scenario
- Methods of detecting discharges
- Detailed containment and disposal plans for discharge cleanups
- Preparedness audits, including records of training, exercises, and drills
- Diagrams showing the facility's topography, including evacuation routes and drainage flow
- Security measures
- A cover sheet that summarizes the facility information

Spill Prevention, Countermeasures, and Control Plan

The Environmental Protection Agency (EPA) has put an emphasis on reducing the risk of oil spills in the environment. To that end, the EPA has leveraged the Clean Water Act (CWA) to guard against oil releases into bodies of water. The **Spill Prevention, Countermeasures, and Control (SPCC) plan** and the facility response plan (FRP) are a means of reducing the risk of oil spills and their impact on the environment.

The SPCC plan is designed to prevent spilled oil from reaching waterways and shorelines. The SPCC plan establishes procedures, methods, and equipment requirements for addressing potential spills of oil near waterways or drains that discharge into waterways. Non-transportation businesses that drill, produce, store, refine, process, use, or consume oil that may reasonably discharge into a waterway must have an SPCC plan if their aboveground capacity exceeds 1,320 gallons or their underground capacity exceeds 42,000 gallons.

Required Elements

Spill Prevention, Countermeasures, and Control (SPCC) applies to any business that stores large amounts of oil on site and where spills could enter waterways or storm drains that lead to waterways. To reduce the risk of oil contaminating the water, the Environmental Protection Agency (EPA) requires such sites to have an SPCC plan. The plan must describe the following:

- Operating procedures used on site to prevent spills, which may include storing or managing the oil in smaller containers
- **Control measures**, such as secondary containment systems, berms, and devices on storm drains, that are used to prevent any spills from reaching water
- Procedures for quickly and effectively responding to spills to contain and clean the spill and to mitigate the impact on the environment

If the facility stores less than 10,000 gallons of oil above ground and has not had a spill that has exceeded 1,000 gallons in the previous three years, they can **self-certify** their SPCC plan. If they do not meet that criteria, the SPCC plan can be prepared by the facility but must be certified by an engineer.

Managing Chemical Spills

The fate of spilled chemicals is dependent on the physical properties of the material. Liquids, by their nature, will flow until they reach physical barriers. Thus, the movement of a liquid can be controlled or halted using berms, dikes, and socks. Chemicals with low boiling points or high **vapor pressure** will evaporate into the atmosphere. These types of chemicals may be best managed by allowing them to evaporate. Solids will remain in a fixed location unless carried by wind or physically moved to another location. Thus, solid spills can typically be removed using shovels, scoops, and brooms.

For spills that contact water, the solubility of the material will determine how to control the spread and remove it from the exposed medium. **Insoluble** solids and liquids (termed "**non-miscible**") can be filtered from the water or skimmed from the surface. Liquids and solids that have a higher density than water, such as chlorinated solvents, may need to be dredged from the bottom of the waterway. **Soluble** solids and liquids (called **miscible**) will require the entire body of water to be treated as the chemical cannot be easily separated from the water.

Physical Methods to Contain or Manage Chemical Spills or Releases

Liquid or solid chemical spills must be contained and cleaned up quickly to keep the chemical from spreading over a larger area. Small liquid spills can be physically contained using absorbent pads or socks or by applying granular **absorbent** to the liquid. Larger spills can be controlled with booms or berms. The liquid can be **siphoned** from the containment area and packaged as hazardous waste while the residue is treated in the same manner as a small spill. Spills that contact soil will require that the contaminated soil be removed as hazardous waste. The volume of soil requiring management will depend on the spread of the material as well as the mobility of the material through the soil.

Solid and liquid spills that contact bodies of water will require similar treatment. If the chemical is not miscible with water, skimming or siphoning it off from the surface may be possible, while liquids that are heavier than water may require dredging to mitigate. Liquids that are miscible with water or solids that are soluble will require more extensive management and mitigation, which could include removing the water from the location or treating the water and installing monitoring equipment to operate over the long term.

Clean Air Act Section 112(r) Accidental Release Program

In response to numerous deadly and costly toxic chemical releases, the Clean Air Act was amended to include a new section, designated **112(r)** and referred to as the "**Accidental Release Program** rule." This section requires sites that store or use regulated substances at or above the specified threshold quantity to prepare a plan to reduce the chance of accidental releases and implement measures to reduce the impact of any such releases. The emphasis of this program is on prevention.

The rule requires facilities that store or use regulated substances at or above their corresponding threshold quantities to conduct a hazard assessment for worst-case-scenario releases, provide a five-year summary of releases, create an accidental release prevention program, design an emergency response plan, and develop a risk management program, which is provided to state and local agencies.

Recovery Plans

Business Continuity Plan

A **business continuity plan** is a document that outlines the process for a business to recover from an unplanned event, such as a natural disaster or chemical release. The plan should include elements addressing when it is to be implemented, assigning authority for initiating and terminating the plan, identifying critical systems, outlining the emergency response itself, identifying resources necessary for recovery, and delineating a method to test the plan prior to an emergency. The plan also identifies who in the organization is responsible for recovering systems and supply chains, lists external vendors or contractors to provide support, and prioritizes systems to return the business to productivity as soon as possible.

The goal of the plan is to reduce unanticipated downtime by reacting to emergencies quickly and efficiently in order to get back to servicing customers as soon as possible.

Emergency Response Plan

An emergency response plan (ERP) is the employer's process for responding to the unintended release of a hazardous material. The ERP can be part of an organization's **contingency plan** but differs in that it is specific for those employers who will have employees respond to the release in some fashion. The extent of the program and training required for staff under the Hazardous Waste Operations and Emergency Response (HAZWOPER) standard will depend on whether employees will simply prevent entry to the release area or actively try to stop the release, leak, or spill.

At a minimum, ERPs should include the following:

- Pre-emergency planning and coordination with local emergency response agencies
- Identifying staff who will respond to the spill, and the required training for such staff
- How staff will recognize a release and the actions they are to take
- Establishing safe distances and places of refuge
- How site security will be established and maintained during emergency activities
- Decontamination procedures for contaminated staff and emergency responders
- Emergency medical treatment and first aid, including coordination with local hospitals
- The procedures used to alert staff and initiate a response
- A method for post-response critique for continual improvement

Preparation

If a project requires hazardous materials to be stored or used on site, the employer must prepare an emergency response plan to reduce any potential harm that may be caused by a release. The ability to respond quickly and stabilize an emergency requires planning, practicing, evaluating, and adjusting.

- Planning – Creating an emergency response plan in advance of an emergency is critical in managing the event. Planning allows roles and responsibilities to be established and necessary materials to be procured before they are needed. The overall goal of planning is to reduce the time between the event and the mitigation to minimize losses.
- Practicing – Response team members must learn to use equipment, ask questions about their roles, and troubleshoot the response plan elements before an actual emergency occurs. Practicing and training is the most effective method for team members to learn to work together without the stress of a real emergency.

- Evaluating – The effectiveness of a plan must be continually evaluated. Practicing an emergency response allows the team to identify areas for improvement before an emergency occurs. Even robust plans must be evaluated after an emergency response. Evaluation should include identifying aspects that worked well, areas that can be improved, and elements that failed to work as designed.
- Adjusting – The plan should be adjusted whenever possible improvements are identified. Response activities that worked well can be expanded to other aspects of the response. Areas that need correction can be adjusted and then practiced again to determine if the performance goals were achieved.

Root Cause Analysis

Goal

A **root cause analysis** is a method used to identify the fundamental reason an incident occurred. There are numerous **formal processes** (fault tree analysis, failure modes analysis, fishbone diagrams, etc.) to assist in identifying the root cause. Direct and indirect causes may be uncovered during the process. The **direct cause** is that condition or action that resulted in the negative event. A drum that fell from a forklift carrying a pallet of solvent is the direct cause of a chemical spill. **Indirect causes** are those conditions that allowed the direct cause to exist. The forklift operator not securing the drums with straps indirectly resulted in the spill. Causes can be categorized as related to equipment, environment, personnel, and management. Once a root cause has been identified, a corrective action can be implemented to prevent the incident from happening in the future.

Methods to Conduct Analysis

Post-incident analysis should involve a root cause analysis to avoid future occurrences. One method available is the **five whys** method. In this method, the problem is identified. Then, questions beginning with "why" are repeatedly asked until the root cause is elucidated. By repeatedly inquiring as to the reason behind an action, circumstance, or result, the user can drive down to the fundamental cause of the problem. Such a method is simple and straightforward and can be applied to hazardous materials releases. The method does not require the iteration occur five times as the root cause may be identified with more or fewer inquiries.

For example, consider the scenario of a post-incident evaluation of a chemical release involving the leak of a 55-gallon drum containing waste oil. The process would be as follows:

- Why did the drum leak? The drum leaked because it had a hole.
- Why did the drum have a hole? The hole was caused by rust.
- Why was there rust on the drum? The rust came from storing the drums outside in the rain.
- Why are the drums in the rain? There is no cover to protect them from getting wet.
- Solution: Place drums under a cover to reduce the impact of water on the drums. Inspect the drums for rust prior to using for waste storage.

Remediation

Spill Kinetics

Identifying Hazardous Chemicals Involved in Spills or Releases

To determine the impact of a chemical release, the identity of the substances involved must be determined. Container labels, transport container placards, UN codes, Environmental Protection Agency (EPA) waste codes, and knowledge of the process that resulted in the release can provide information on what has entered the environment. Additionally, laboratory analysis of air, water, or soil samples can provide information on both the type of chemical involved in the release and the level of contamination. This analytical process is referred to as environmental sampling.

Environmental Sampling Techniques

Environmental sampling is the collection of data regarding the types chemical contaminants present in a particular area and the level of contamination in that area. Sampling provides more reliable data than modeling as it eliminates any assumptions or input areas when determining the concentrations of chemicals at various locations. Sampling techniques fall into one of three general categories:

- **Field screening** – Real-time tests allow investigators to obtain rough estimates of contaminant levels and identify areas of potentially high or low concentration. These tests are well suited for providing preliminary information and guiding future analytical planning. Examples include colorimetric indicator tubes and multi-gas meters.
- **Field laboratory** – Using more robust and expensive instrumentation than that used in screening techniques, field laboratories provide results that are more accurate and precise. The results obtained may be as reliable as laboratory results but may not be of similar quality due to the non-ideal conditions in which the laboratories typically operate. Portable gas chromatographs and infrared spectrometers are analytical tools that can be used in the field.
- **Stationary laboratory** – Samples collected in the field are sent to a laboratory for analysis. Stationary laboratories provide the most accurate and reliable data. However, this technique relies on proper sample collection, packaging, and storage to ensure that the sample received by the laboratory represents the conditions at the site. Stationary laboratories typically provide a broader spectrum of analysis than portable equipment and are more accurate than screening techniques.

Sampling Plan in Remediation Projects

A **sampling plan** or **sampling design** is a detailed outline of which environmental samples will be collected from a site being investigated. It contains information on the location, depth, medium, and amount of samples collected. The intent of a sampling plan is to make sure that the totality of the analytical results provides a representation of the site conditions and the spread of contamination. The sampling plan is critical in determining the extent of the migration of all contaminants of interest. Sampling plans should include a map of the area to provide context for each sample's location and relation to other samples.

Sampling Designs for Chemical Releases

There are several types of sampling design strategies that the Environmental Protection Agency (EPA) has identified for general sampling projects. However, three sampling designs may be particularly well suited for environmental contamination projects:

- **Random** – In this sampling design, samples are collected within a specified area, but with no bias or consideration of other factors.
- **Systematic and grid** – The area is divided into equal segments and a sample is collected from each segment regardless of other information, such as proximity to the release.
- **Judgmental** – Professional knowledge and experience are used in conjunction with site-specific information (such as topography and location) to select sampling locations.

Movement of Spilled Materials Through the Environment

A critical factor in determining how a chemical migrates through the environment is the physical properties of the material. The horizontal and vertical movement of the material is dependent on these properties. Downward vertical movement through the soil is typically based on **water solubility**, with soluble chemicals being carried further into the soil by surface water. As the water soaks into the soil and migrates toward any groundwater, a process referred to as "leaching," it carries water-soluble chemicals with it. Leaching may also increase the underground horizontal movement of the chemical. Water-soluble chemicals will travel further and deeper than those which are not soluble in water.

Upward vertical movement from a spill will be dependent on both vapor pressure and boiling point of the material as it evaporates into the air. Horizontal movement will depend on both the physical state of the material (with solids moving much less than liquids) and the water solubility (with water-soluble chemicals moving via surface waters and runoff).

Movement of Contaminated Groundwater Through the Soil

Both solid and liquid hazardous chemicals can be carried into the soil by surface waters. If the material is water soluble, it can dissolve in the water and be carried deep into the soil. The depth of penetration depends on the soil type and soil condition in the area of the spill. Porous or loosely packed soils will allow water to **percolate** deeper than tightly packed soils or clay. Underground rock formations may have cracks or **fissures** that will allow the groundwater to penetrate further into the soil. On the contrary, if there are clay deposits or dense soil layers, these will act as barriers to water penetration. These barriers will increase the horizontal spread of the contaminated water through the area.

Migration of Non-Water-Soluble Liquids Through Water

Non-water-soluble liquids, such as petroleum products and halogenated chemicals, can contaminate aboveground and underground bodies of water even though they do not mix with the liquid.

Leaking underground tanks or spilled liquids can release chemicals that percolate through porous soils by the action of gravity. Once they come into contact with an underground aquifer, the **mechanical action** of the moving water will cause the material to spread. Spills that enter storm drains or surface waters will travel with any water present and spread contamination. Liquids that are less dense than water, such as petroleum products, will float on the surface of the water while halogenated hydrocarbons will sink.

Spill Remediation Objectives

Remediation

A physical area can become polluted with a hazardous chemical as a result of industrial activities at that location, intentional application of chemicals (such as pesticides or fertilizers) in large amounts, or accidents involving chemicals. Remediation is the process of removing chemical pollutants from the impacted soil and water at these locations as well as locations that may be impacted by the movement of chemicals through the environment, as by contaminating groundwater.

Remediation Project

A remediation project is implemented in response to a known or suspected contamination of soil or water with a hazardous chemical. The chemical has escaped containment and reached levels in the environment where it can negatively impact health or the plants and animals in the affected area. The objectives of any remediation project are to reduce the level of all hazardous chemicals to protect human health and to restore the environment back to a healthy, nonpolluted state. Depending on the substance, a remediation project may not completely eliminate the chemical from the environment, but it may reduce it to a level that does not harm human, animal, or plant health.

Preliminary Remediation Goals

A chemical spill results in hazardous substances entering the environment, causing **measurable levels** above established **acceptable thresholds**. When a site is undergoing remediation to address a specific hazardous chemical, there needs to be a target value below which no additional treatment is necessary. A **preliminary remediation goal (PRG)** is an average concentration value at a site undergoing remediation below which an individual exposed at random in the area of concern is within the **acceptable risk level**. If the average value within the exposure area is below the PRG, remediation is no longer required. If the value exceeds the PRG, remediation needs to continue, or another remediation technique needs to be implemented.

RCRA Corrective Action Program

When a facility has a chemical release, the **Corrective Action program (CAP)** under the Resource Conservation and Recovery Act (RCRA) provides the framework for the cleanup. The program applies to any release in the air, water, or soil. The CAP is typically required under a treatment, storage, and disposal facility (TSDF) permit. The program is designed to investigate releases, determine the scope of the release, and identify a treatment strategy to reduce the identified contaminants below regulatory levels.

Elements

The Resource Conservation and Recovery Act (RCRA) Corrective Action program is results-based and flexible, and considers the specifics of any incident. Thus, the process does not involve sequential steps as much as evaluations, only some of which must occur before another can begin. The seven elements in the Corrective Action program are as follows:

- **RCRA Facility Assessment (RFA)** – an initial assessment of environmental conditions to determine if a release occurred
- **RCRA Facility Investigation (RFI)** – a site characterization which assesses the scope and scale of the contamination, including identifying the presence, movement, fate, and risks of hazardous chemicals in the environment
- Interim actions – steps taken while the RFI is being completed and before a final resolution is selected

- **Corrective Action Measures Study (CMS)** – an evaluation of the advantages and disadvantages of the available corrective actions
- **Corrective Measure Implementation (CMI)** – once a remedy is identified, it must be designed, constructed, operated, maintained, and, completed
- Tracking progress – periodic reports to the state agency overseeing the remediation, providing updates on conditions and progress
- Long-term care – controls implemented to ensure that the remediation was successful and that future exposures are minimized

Spill Remediation Technology

Capital Cost and Recurring Costs in Remediation Activities

A **capital cost** is a fixed, one-time purchase, typically involving property, buildings, or equipment. For example, a remediation project involving groundwater would have capital costs of drilling a well, purchasing a pump, and installing a pump system.

Recurring costs are expenditures that occur at regular intervals. Recurring costs include **operation and maintenance (O&M)** costs, which are the dollars spent running a process. In the groundwater example, O&M costs would include routine inspection and maintenance of the pump system.

When selecting a remediation technology, the responsible party is interested in comparing the cost and effectiveness of the available options. The evaluation must consider both the capital cost and the recurring costs when considering the potential financial outlay, balanced with a consideration of the expected contaminant reduction and expected timeframe.

Considerations with Remediation Cost Estimates

In determining the potential costs of remediation, the responsible party must contract with experienced companies that perform this type of work. However, as with any financial proposal project, the responsible party must be aware of the limitations of an **environmental remediation cost estimate**. One of the primary considerations is that each site is unique, and the contractor will invariably run into problems at the location of the remediation that were not considered or could not be considered during the estimate process. Secondly, it may be difficult to directly compare costs from different vendors because of differences in their cost-reporting metrics. It is difficult to compare a bid expressed as dollars per volume treated to one based on contaminant reduction levels to another that uses surface area treated. A third consideration is that the estimate may not include variable costs. Such costs include necessary permits, equipment transport costs, or site-specific system modifications (such as stabilizers or pontoons).

Capital Costs for Environmental Remediation Projects

When comparing bids or budgeting for an environmental remediation project, the planners must take into consideration both one-time (capital) costs and recurring (operations and maintenance) costs to select the most cost-effective option. For any project, capital costs to be evaluated should include the following:

- Site preparation – including any vegetation clearing, access road construction, drilling, permits, fencing, and utility installation.
- Structures – any buildings or platforms that need to be constructed or rented
- Process equipment – the equipment required for the actual remediation

- Non-process equipment – support equipment, including computers, vehicles, and safety equipment
- Utilities – the cost of running conduit, pipes, and wires for utilities required at the site
- Labor costs – labor required for the installation, setup, and testing of the process equipment
- Other costs – any other one-time costs, such as equipment rentals for installation and setup

Recurring Costs for Environmental Remediation Projects

In addition to one-time costs, recurring costs (including operation and maintenance, or O&M), must be evaluated when selecting a contractor for a remediation project. Recurring costs include the following:

- Direct labor cost - including salary and benefits for laborers and supervisory staff operating or maintaining the remediation process equipment
- Direct materials – consumables used by the process, such as carbon filters, screeds, chemical wash solutions, and replacement parts
- Overhead – insurance, equipment maintenance contracts, waste shipping charges, operation equipment rental, and licensing
- General and administrative – project management costs, stakeholder communication (to keep the public or other parties informed of progress), travel costs, etc.
- Site management – waste disposal costs, health and safety equipment, site closure activities, and sample analysis costs

Spill Treatment

Treatment Technologies for Contaminated Groundwater

Before treatment can begin, the source of any spill or release must be controlled or removed to stop an increase in concentration. Once the release has been addressed, the media must be treated to lower the concentration of the pollutant and return it to a more natural state. For contaminated groundwater, there are four generally accepted treatment methods:

- Containing the contaminated groundwater to prevent it from migrating through the environment
- Pumping the water out of the aquifer, treating it above the ground, and pumping the water back into the aquifer
- Treating the aquifer underground
- Allowing natural processes, including dilution, to continue until the level has achieved the desired standard while taking measures to ensure the contaminated water does not lead to an exposure (such as finding an alternate source of drinking water until the process has run its course)

There are numerous treatment methods for aboveground and belowground treatment of groundwater, including thermal treatment, air sparging, chemical treatment, or carbon filtering.

Treatment Technologies for Contaminated Soil

The intent of treating soil contaminated with hazardous chemicals is to prevent the materials moving to uncontaminated media, such as clean soil, water, or air. Soil treatment technologies fall into six categories:

- Containment – removing the contaminated soil and disposing of it in appropriate containers to prevent chemicals leaching from the material
- Washing – removing chemicals by passing water or other liquids through the soil to dissolve the contaminant
- **Thermal treatment** – applying heat to contaminated soil to evaporate off chemicals that have lower boiling temperatures (also referred to as "thermal desorption")
- **Vapor extraction** – placing contaminated soil in a unit that uses vacuum pressure to remove volatile chemicals
- **Bioremediation** – using microorganisms that feed on specific contaminants to clean the soil
- Incineration – thermally treating contaminated soil in a furnace (typically used for soils contaminated with heavy hydrocarbons)

Fugitive Air Release

Any discharge resulting from an equipment leak, releases from ventilation systems, pressure release discharges, and evaporative losses from waste treatment units, such as surface impoundments and spills, are referred to as "**fugitive air releases**." Typically, harmful fugitive air emissions cannot be treated, and the only mitigation technique may be to model the migration of the emission, monitor the concentration within the predicted area, and manage affected populations properly, either by evacuating or issuing shelter-in-place orders.

Site-Specific Soil Screening Levels

Site-specific soil screening levels (SSLs) are calculated values used to determine if a location requires additional remediation. SSLs are devised by environmental engineers using standardized equations with exposure assumptions and Environmental Protection Agency (EPA) toxicity data. Generic SSLs are available for common environmental contaminants. They are not federal standards and do not infer that remediation is required. They are used to guide remediation efforts and to monitor progress. If soil analysis sample results fall below the SSL, then no further action or evaluation is required.

Evaluating Impact of Groundwater Remediation Strategies

Under the Comprehensive Environmental Response, Compensation, and Liability Act (CERCLA), Congress established that groundwater remediation can stop once the contaminants in the aquifer are reduced to **levels** established under the Clean Water Act. The residual water must achieve the **maximum containment level goals (MCLGs)** under the **Safe Drinking Water Act** for remediation to be considered complete. An MCLG is the maximum level at which a given contaminant has no known adverse health effects on the population and can be deemed safe.

Redevelopment Considerations and Pitfalls

Redeveloping Sites Remediated After a Chemical Release

After cleanup, a site that has been involved in a chemical release and subsequent remediation can be considered for **redevelopment**. Redevelopment reduces community blight by finding uses for abandoned or unused properties. Depending on the location of the property, the project could be used for infill, helping to reduce urban sprawl. Converting a project from an industrial use to another use can increase the tax base of the municipality, resulting in additional revenue. If a remediation site is converted into a park or open space, it will increase the greenspace available to the community.

Risks Associated with Reusing Former Remediation Sites

The sale or reuse of former cleanup sites has associated risks that need to be considered before a final determination is made on their use. In rare instances, the cleanup may not have addressed all contamination, in which case there is a risk of **liability** for any health conditions that could be related to exposure at the location. Additionally, the question of long-term monitoring must be addressed before any real estate transaction can occur. Prospective developers may have to navigate changing timelines if the remediation is still in progress. Lenders may have concerns regarding providing financing for former contaminated properties due to the unknown status of title and cleanup responsibility. Finally, if the site is known in the community, the stigma of the location may last well beyond the removal of remediation equipment.

Soil Remediation Standards

Fates of Contaminated Soil

Soil that has been contaminated with a hazardous chemical as a result of a release, spill, or accumulation over time can be managed in one of two ways— disposal as a hazardous waste or remediation and return to its native location.

Soil that is to be managed as a hazardous waste must be evaluated to determine if it is subject to the Land Disposal Restriction (LDR) program and must therefore undergo some level of treatment before disposal.

Soil that is to be returned to the site from where it was removed must be treated in such a way that all contaminants are reduced to the original (i.e., background) levels.

Alternative Soil Treatment Standard

Contaminated soil that will be disposed of must meet the standards under the Resource Conservation and Recovery Act (RCRA) Land Disposal Restriction (LDR) standard. For soil, RCRA has established two alternative soil treatment standards that must be met before a soil can be disposed of in a landfill. The standard compares the initial concentration of a contaminant to the post-treatment concentration. The treatment technology must reduce the concentration to a level that is 90 percent less than the initial concentration, or to a level not more than 10 times the amount listed in the **universal treatment standard** (listed in 40 CFR 268.48), whichever is greater.

Determining When Contaminated Soil Is No Longer Hazardous

Contaminated soil must have all hazardous contaminants removed. If the soil is to be disposed of in a permitted landfill, contaminant levels must be reduced below the Land Disposal Restriction (LDR) limits. Soil that has been treated is referred to as "**residual.**" Per the **derived-from rule** of the Environmental Protection Agency, any material derived from a hazardous waste is still considered hazardous if the waste itself is listed. In the event of a characteristic waste, the residual is only considered hazardous if it exhibits a hazardous characteristic (e.g., toxic, flammable, corrosive). Thus, soil that no longer exhibits a hazardous waste characteristic is no longer considered hazardous and does not need to be managed as such.

Management Systems

Multimedia Program Regulations

Multimedia Site Inspection

A **multimedia inspection** evaluates a facility's overall compliance with regulations as opposed to being focused on a single topic. Multimedia inspections may be environmental in nature or related to health and safety. A multimedia inspection may also evaluate performance issues, such as pollution prevention, and such evaluation may be above and beyond the regulatory standard. For example, an environmental multimedia inspection may evaluate air emissions, hazardous waste storage, and potential water discharges. The intent of such an inspection is to limit business interruptions by consolidating multiple inspections by several inspectors into a single visit by a single evaluator.

Reducing a Company's Exposure During Inspection

A multimedia inspection that evaluates compliance with multiple regulations can be daunting for a business. However, advance preparation using a four-step process can reduce the organization's exposure and reduce potential noncompliance findings. The process is as follows:

- Step 1: Noncompliance identification – Internal audits can assist the organization in identifying where it needs to improve or achieve compliance. Multiple audits covering all regulatory exposures will provide a comprehensive picture of where the organization stands.
- Step 2: External audits – Regulatory agencies have programs wherein they can request audits that are nonpunitive in nature, designed to assist the business in identifying areas of noncompliance before a violation or fine is issued. This is a cooperative effort between the agency and industry to reduce penalties and work toward the overall goal of injury reduction and pollution reduction.
- Step 3: Implement compliance programs – After deficiencies have been identified, the organization must prioritize and address the means to achieve compliance with all applicable regulations.
- Step 4: Employee preparation – Now that the programs have been implemented, the employees need to be engaged. Training on all changes or modifications should be conducted.

Determining Programs for Implementation

To determine what programs are applicable to a specific facility, the employer must evaluate all processes and functions that occur on site. A facility inspection will assist in identifying such things as hazardous waste storage, water discharges, air emissions, and chemical usage. Once the activities are identified, the employer must research applicable standards for the required environmental programs and health and safety programs. All identified standards must be reviewed to determine if they apply to the business and what the requirements are. Finally, all programs must be developed, written, and implemented to achieve compliance.

Record Maintenance and Retention Requirements

Reportable and Recordable Injuries

The Occupational Safety and Health Administration (OSHA) requires nonexempt employers to maintain records of occupational injuries. In some instances, the employer must report the injury to OSHA within a certain timeframe. Thus, OSHA distinguishes between recordable and reportable injuries.

A **recordable injury** is any work-related injury that results in death, loss of consciousness, days away from work, restricted work due to the injury, transfer to another job due to the injury, or any injury that requires medical treatment beyond first aid, including fractures, burst eardrums, chronic illnesses including cancer, or broken teeth. Records must be kept if the facility falls under the scope of the OSHA recordkeeping standard.

A **reportable injury** is where the employer must directly contact OSHA and notify them of the situation. An employer has eight hours to report any fatality to their regional office. An employer has 24 hours to report any work-related amputation (loss of bone) or loss of an eye, or to report that an employee has been admitted to a hospital for treatment. All employers must report these injuries, regardless of whether they are required to maintain records of injuries. All reportable injuries are recordable, but not all recordable injuries are reportable.

OSHA's Injury Recordkeeping Requirements

The Occupational Safety and Health Administration (OSHA) requires that an employer maintain records of all recordable injuries unless the employer is exempt under the **recordkeeping rule**. The employer must record qualifying injuries on a **Form 300** (or state equivalent). These records must be maintained for five years, after which they may be destroyed. Each year, from February 1 to April 30, the employer must post a **Form 300A**, which is a summary of all injuries recorded on Form 300 for the prior year.

Recordkeeping for Employee Exposure to Hazardous Material

Exposures to hazardous materials may result in latent health effects, meaning the effects do not develop for many years. Thus, whenever there is an employee exposure, the Occupational Safety and Health Administration requires that employers retain employee medical records related to work-related exposures for the duration of employment plus 30 years.

Additionally, any air monitoring records that were taken when an employee exposure occurred must also be kept for 30 years. Air monitoring records include the sampling plan, the sample analysis results, any mathematical or analytical methods used, and a summary of any background data used to determine the exposure level. Along with the air monitoring records, the safety data sheet for the material must also be retained for the same amount of time.

Need for Recordkeeping Under OSHA Standards

The Occupational Safety and Health Administration (OSHA) uses records to demonstrate whether an employer is adhering to a regulation. During a site visit, the OSHA inspector will likely request records relevant to the issue they are investigating. A facility that does not have records cannot demonstrate compliance, which can result in violations and associated fines.

Records include written programs, training logs, training programs, sampling data, waste transportation documents, and other proof that regulations were being followed appropriately. Typically, OSHA allows records to be maintained electronically, but they must be available to the inspector upon request. The employer must review all relevant standards to determine what records must be kept and for how long.

Review and Interpretation of Regulations

The Federal Register and the Code of Federal Regulations

The **Federal Register (FR)** is a daily publication of the federal government. The FR is the method by which the government meets the **public notification requirements** of its rulemaking process. The FR contains federal agency notices, presidential executive orders, proposed rules, and final rules. Once a final rule has been published in the FR and the comment period has passed, the rule becomes codified in the **Code of Federal Regulations (CFR)** and then has the power of law.

Determining If Regulation Is Current

The **Government Publishing Office (GPO)** publishes and maintains the Code of Federal Regulations (CFR). The CFR covers 50 titles and is published annually. Due to the volume of material, the CFR is updated quarterly in parts: Titles 1–16 on January 1, Titles 17–27 on April 1, Titles 28–41 on July 1, and Titles 42–50 on October 1. The date of revision is included on each standard. For example, Occupational Safety and Health Administration (OSHA) standards are located in Title 29 of the CFR while Environmental Protection Agency (EPA) standards are located in Title 40. At the bottom of each standard, there is a **revision history** with the most recent revision listed last.

Currently, the CFR is also published in an electronic format, the eCFR, through the GPO website. The most recent upload date is listed on each page of the eCFR.

Regulation Development

Laws and Regulations

Laws are proposed by Congress and approved by the President. Starting as a bill, a law is discussed by the two houses of Congress, who must agree on common language for the bill. The bill is then forwarded to the President, who can either sign or veto the bill. If it is signed, it is added to the **United States Code (USC)** as a law (also called an "act" or a "statute"). The USC is published in its entirety every six years, with annual supplements published to keep the information current. Laws typically lack specific details or require additional information for application. For example, the Clean Air Act (CAA) requires the Environmental Protection Agency (EPA) to develop a list of hazardous air pollutants, and the CAA itself does not list them.

A regulation is proposed by a governmental agency to provide specific guidance on how to meet the requirements of a law. Under the CAA, the EPA established regulations for specific air contaminants and maximum emission levels for each contaminant. Regulations consider input from stakeholders prior to being finalized. Regulations under development or recently completed are published annually under each government agency's regulatory agenda and regulatory plans.

Creating a Regulation

A regulation undergoes a four-step process prior to being codified in the Code of Federal Regulations. First, the applicable agency must determine whether a new regulation is necessary or the same goals can be achieved under a current regulation. If a new regulation is determined to be appropriate, the next step is to develop the proposed regulation and publish it in the Federal Register for **public comment**. Third, public comments are reviewed and considered for potential revisions. Finally, the revised regulation is published in the Federal Register as a final rule, after which it becomes enforceable as part of the Code of Federal Regulations.

Knowledge Base Needed to Participate in EPA Regulation Development

The **Office of Policy (OP)** of the Environmental Protection Agency (EPA) manages the regulatory development process. Under the OP, the EPA created the Smart Sector program. This program is a partnership with trade associations that will be affected by pending regulations or changes to existing regulations.

Any member of the public, including members of the industries that would be impacted by proposed rules, can comment on proposed rules. The government has established an electronic portal (regulations.gov) as the forum for publishing comments on proposed rules.

Means by Which New Regulations Are Proposed

Governmental agencies are the entities responsible for identifying and developing new regulations. An agency may determine that a new regulation is necessary using several sources. A new law may require a regulation, a series of related accidents or other impacts on society may necessitate a rule change, stakeholders may petition for a new rule, or agency staff may recommend a new rule. Once the determination has been made that a new regulation may be appropriate, the regulation goes through the development process.

Requirements for Participating in Rulemaking Process

Once the need for a rule is established, a proposal is published in the federal government's annual **Unified Agenda**, which includes all upcoming rulemaking for the year. The agency responsible for a new rule will publish the **Regulatory Plan** in the Federal Register. The plan establishes the timeline for the rulemaking. Additionally, an **Advance Notice of Proposed Rulemaking** may be published in the Federal Register. In either instance, any interested party (an individual or a group) may submit comments to develop the rule, improve the draft of the rule, or argue against the rule. If an agency uses a process of **negotiated rulemaking**, they may invite members of stakeholder groups to directly participate in the rulemaking meetings.

Public Outreach for Standard Development

Informing the Public of Pending Regulatory Change

Public participation in the regulatory development process can provide two benefits. First, the agency promulgating the regulation will make decisions that are better aligned with the public interest and values. This will facilitate implementation and public understanding. Second, the public process will allow the community not only to understand the function of the agency but also to develop problem-solving strategies that align with the agency's goals. With the information exchange that occurs, both the agency and the public obtain a higher level of understanding of the problem itself as well as the impact of proposed solutions.

Public information can be presented either individually or by mass communication. Individual modes include meetings, briefings, and telephone calls. Modes of mass communication include printed information, websites, hotlines, and press releases. All modes have benefits and drawbacks that must be considered before one is utilized.

Public Comment Requirements for Development of Regulations

The federal rulemaking process requires that the public be provided an opportunity to review proposed regulations or changes and to comment on them or provide other supplemental information that could impact the final rule.

Proposed rules and changes must be published in the Federal Register to meet the public notification requirement. Proposed rules and changes will have a public comment period, ranging from 30 to 180 days, depending on the complexity and potential impact of the rule. Comments are submitted electronically and considered by the agency promulgating the change. Agencies may also elect to hold public hearings to allow for additional comments.

Stakeholders and Communication

Stakeholder

A **stakeholder** is any party that has an interest in the business activities of an organization or entity because the party either affects or is affected by the organization's activities. **Internal stakeholders** are groups within the business, including the employees, management, and investors. **External stakeholders** are entities outside of the business that have an actual or perceived impact from the operations. They can be customers, individuals in the community, groups such as youth teams that use a nearby park or a nearby community association, fire departments, government regulatory agencies, or nearby businesses.

Importance of Communicating with Stakeholders

Communication is the transfer of information from one party to another. Communicating with stakeholders serves many purposes, including building relationships, informing, and managing information. Businesses that regularly and voluntarily communicate can build successful relationships with their stakeholders. They appear to be forthcoming and more transparent than businesses who rarely communicate. A deliberate **communication plan** can help the business manage rumors and negative incidents rather than merely reacting to information that they do not control. The level of communication should be tailored to the specific audience to be effective.

In business, stakeholder communication must be two-way to be successful. Not only must a business keep their stakeholders appropriately informed, but they must also listen. Customers can provide insight into new opportunities, community groups can provide routes forward for projects or help determine solutions, and conversations with government agencies can assist in long-term regulatory planning.

Communication with Internal Stakeholders

Internal communication is a critical element of any management system. Informing employees of projects, plans, forecasts, accidents, and incidents builds trust and support within the organization. A lack of communication allows rumors to spread and can create a negative environment. Organizations can convey information to internal stakeholders by way of in-person meetings or briefings, conference calls with remote parties, regular newsletters, postings in common areas, and announcements over PA systems. The mode of communicating should be selected based on the information to be conveyed, taking into consideration the necessary audience, the sensitivity of the information, the benefit of feedback, and the need for clarity to prevent misunderstandings or confusion.

Types of Communication with External Stakeholders

Information required by external stakeholders varies depending on the group the external stakeholders are in, their role in or impact on the business, and the expected result from the communication. Communication to a regulatory agency will be different in content, context, mode, and message than a presentation to a community group. There are four broad categories of means of communicating with external stakeholders:

- **Earned media** – free exposure in media that the business does not pay for (including radio and television as well as and news outlet interviews, articles, op-eds, and editorials)
- **Paid media** – exposure in media that is paid for by the organization (including print ads, news releases, mailers, and billboards, which all have costs that must be weighed against the benefits)
- **New media** – exposure on electronic media, such as blogs, social networks, and webpages
- **Events** – presentations, such as rallies or other events that are informational only; interactive events, such as community forums, roundtables, or press conferences, which generally allow for questions from the audience

Management System Audits vs. Compliance Audits

Objective of Audits

An **audit** is a systematic review of records and documents. The objective of an audit is to evaluate whether an organization is adhering to regulations, policies, and procedures. These can include both external regulations, such as hazardous waste management requirements, or internal regulations, such as payroll policies. Auditors may issue corrective actions that identify areas of noncompliance where the organization needs to improve or change to achieve compliance.

Compliance Audit

In health and safety programs, there are two main types of audits–a compliance audit and a management system audit. A **compliance audit** determines if the organization is adhering to local, state, and federal regulations. The audit may be vertical, focusing on a single topic (such as a groundwater monitoring program), or horizontal, surveying all regulations that apply to a particular process. A compliance audit seeks to locate areas of noncompliance with a standard, such as not having a written respiratory protection program. The result of a compliance audit is typically a corrective action to bring operations back into alignment with standards.

Management System Audit

A **management system audit** evaluates whether an organization is adhering to an **industry standard** or **best practice**. While not legally enforceable like regulations, industry standards can provide an organization with a competitive advantage if followed, such as by being ISO 9001 quality system certified. The management system audit relies on objective evidence to demonstrate that processes required under the standard of interest are in place. As with compliance audits, areas of nonconformance are identified for correction; however, a system audit will also note areas of conformance. Findings from system audits are not intended to correct an identified issue but are instead geared toward building a better system.

Cost-Benefit Analysis Variables

Cost-Benefit Analysis

A **cost-benefit analysis** is a way for an organization to make an evidence-based decision by considering the financial perspective of the proposed action. The process compares the **hard costs** and **soft costs** involved in implementing the change, including capital costs and staff time, to the benefits gained through the change. Benefits may be long-term savings, improved quality, reduction in fines assessed, or improved safety. Soft benefits, such as an improvement in employee morale or reputation, can also be assessed if a dollar amount can be attributed to the variable. When all costs and benefits are expressed as dollars, a management team can make a more informed decision.

Variables When Conducting Cost-Benefit Analysis for Environmental Program

Environmental cost-benefit analysis evaluates the impact a change will have on an **environmental management system**, whether it is to equipment, processes, or procedures. In the analysis, soft and hard costs must be compared to the financial and system benefits that would come from a reduction in the frequency or severity of releases.

Cost variables to consider include equipment costs (including replacements, upgrades, and modifications), salary that is required to implement the change or that otherwise results from the change, process impacts on deliverables, materials cost changes (including increased or decreased costs of substitute materials), and any additional regulatory or permit requirements.

Benefits fall into two categories—monetarily **quantifiable** and **nonquantifiable** variables. Monetarily quantifiable benefits include decreases in insurance costs and savings through reducing the use of hazardous materials in the production process. Nonquantifiable variables include an improvement in the organization's image and the lack of an impact on surrounding natural environments.

Written Programs

Requirement for Written Compliance Programs

The burden is on the employer to determine which regulatory programs apply to their business operations. Once an employer identifies the applicable regulations, the regulations must be evaluated for any written program requirements. If a documented program is required, the employer must develop the program and train employees on the components of the program to make sure everyone understands the regulatory requirements. Some businesses may determine that several standards apply, which will require several separate written programs addressing each regulation in turn.

Updating Written Compliance Programs

Regulatory agencies require that compliance programs required under a regulatory standard must be written. This gives every employee the ability to review the document in order to understand both how the employer is complying and what the expectations are for management as well as employees. Additionally, inspectors will request written programs during a site visit to verify that the business is in compliance.

The Occupational Safety and Health Administration (OSHA) requires that health and safety programs undergo annual review. Environmental programs should have a review periodicity established to keep the program updated with any changes in the regulation.

AVAILABILITY REQUIREMENTS FOR WRITTEN COMPLIANCE PROGRAMS

The intent of a written program is to codify how an organization is meeting a set of regulatory requirements. The document also serves as a record of compliance. The Occupational Safety and Health Administration requires that written programs be made available to employees so that they have access to the information. Written programs may be kept electronically, but they must be available upon request from a supervisor or for independent employee access (e.g., not on a server the employee cannot access). Additionally, during a regulatory inspection, the plan must be in a format that can be provided to the inspector upon demand.

Environmental Studies

Property Transfer Environmental Due Diligence

Environmental Due Diligence in Relation to Real Estate Transactions

Environmental **due diligence** is the assessment of known or potential **environmental liabilities** associated with a piece of property. Specifically, the evaluation attempts to identify any chemical contamination on the property (that may require future remediation) as well as the degree of any contamination. The assessment, also referred to as a "**Phase 1 Environmental Site Assessment (ESA)**," looks to identify property attributes and conditions, past uses that may have had environmental impacts, past ownership, and the potential for associated soil or groundwater contamination.

Goals of Environmental Due Diligence Process

Conducting an environmental site assessment (ESA) as part of environmental due diligence allows the property owner, potential buyer, or local municipality to gain an understanding of the condition of the property and any potential liabilities. In conducting such an assessment, the investigating party looks to identify the following:

- Any hazardous substances that may be or have been present on the property.
- Any indications that a chemical release occurred or may occur on the property.
- Inspections or testing of soil, groundwater, surface water, and buildings on the property for the presence of hazardous substances.
- Any past, present, or future cleanup activities necessary under the Comprehensive Environmental Response, Compensation, and Liability Act (CERCLA).
- The regulatory status of the property.
- Parts of the ownership history that may indicate potential environmental concerns.
- Any substances that are currently on the property and the related cleanup actions that would be necessary to remediate the area.

Requirement for Environmental Due Diligence Assessment

Evaluating a property for chemical contamination may be required in certain instances prior to a transaction taking place. A lending institution may require the assessment prior to financing a real estate purchase, refinancing a loan for a property, or accepting the property as collateral for a construction loan. Public agencies may require a due diligence assessment before they release grant funds for developments or improvements on a piece of property. The lender or agency is looking to evaluate future costs or other factors that could impact the transaction or development potential.

Phase I Environmental Site Assessment

An environmental site assessment may be required by lenders or government agencies when property transactions are involved. The Phase I Environmental Site Assessment (ESA) involves research on the current and historical uses of the property that may have resulted in site contamination. A Phase I ESA will look to identify such conditions as the presence of asbestos-containing materials (ACM), the presence of lead-based paint (LBP), mold growth, soil contamination, and water contamination. After all appropriate inquiries have been made, the environmental professional will review the data and issue a report, making recommendations for any remediation actions.

Recognized Environmental Condition, Controlled Recognized Environmental Condition, and Historical Recognized Environmental Condition

A **Phase I Environmental Site Assessment (ESA)** will attempt to identify the known or suspected presence of environmental hazards on a property. The information collected may identify a recognized environmental condition, a controlled recognized environmental condition, or a historical recognized environmental condition. The implications of these conditions are as follows:

- **Recognized environmental condition (REC)** - There is known contamination, or there is a possibility of subsurface contamination on the property.
- **Controlled recognized environmental condition (CREC)** - There has been contamination on or under the property that has been addressed, but additional remediation would be required if the site were to be redeveloped.
- **Historical recognized environmental condition (HREC)** - There was a past release that has been appropriately remediated, and the property has no restrictions on its use.

Phase II Environmental Testing During ESA

A Phase I Environmental Site Assessment (ESA) is used to identify known or suspected contamination at a location involved in a real estate transaction. If a recognized environmental condition (REC) is identified, a **Phase II ESA**—environmental testing—may be requested by a stakeholder. Phase II involves conducting subsurface testing of soil and water to identify the source of the contamination and, if possible, the party liable for remediation. The testing is conducted by specialists, including geologists and engineers, per relevant **ASTM International** standards. Testing allows stakeholders to get a complete picture of the environmental status of a site and the risks of purchasing a site prior to completing the transaction.

"All Appropriate Inquiries" Required to Obtain Liability Protection Under CERCLA for Environmental Due Diligence

To activate the liability protections under the Comprehensive Environmental Response, Compensation, and Liability Act (CERCLA) for a potential property purchase, the prospective buyer must make **all appropriate inquiries** regarding the environmental status of the property. Under the "all appropriate inquiries" rule, no more than 180 days prior to acquiring the property, the interested party must conduct the following inquiries:

- Interviews with past and previous owners or occupiers
- Searches for any current environmental liens
- Reviews of applicable government records for a history of releases or permits that provides information regarding potential chemicals that were on site
- Visual inspections of the subject property and adjacent properties
- An evaluation by an environmental professional

Liability Protection for Prospective Buyer for Potentially Contaminated Property

The Comprehensive Environmental Response, Compensation, and Liability Act (CERCLA) offers protections of persons looking to purchase a contaminated property. Under the **liability protection** clause, the new landowner does not incur the costs of cleaning up the property. Those costs and responsibility for remediation reside with the owner who held the land at the time the release was detected or whose operations resulted in the contamination.

Building Surveys

Regulated Hazardous Building Materials

The Occupational Safety and Health Administration (OSHA) has identified a list of substances that are of such concern that they have been assigned their own specific regulations. These substances are regulated in 29 CFR under Subpart Z. Building construction materials and components may contain some of these regulated hazardous materials. In most instances, these materials pose no hazards if they are left alone. However, repairs, replacements, renovations, and demolition can create situations where employees or contractors must handle or otherwise become exposed to these materials. Examples include asbestos (tiles, fireproofing), lead (paint, solder), PCBs (transformer oil), mercury (fluorescent tubes, thermostats), CFC refrigerants, and silica dust (concrete, stucco, plaster).

Asbestos Hazard Emergency Response Act

The **Asbestos Hazard Emergency Response Act (AHERA)** is a set of laws promulgated by the Environmental Protection Agency (EPA) to mitigate the hazards presented by asbestos. AHERA requires that public and charter schools conduct a survey of their sites to identify the presence and location of possible asbestos-containing materials (ACM). In addition to inspections, AHERA requires that the school prepare plans to reduce or prevent exposure to ACM. The act does not require that action be taken to remove the materials, but it does require schools to provide **awareness training** to custodial staff and annually notify staff, management, and parents of any asbestos-related actions that have occurred. The survey must be updated every three years.

Components of Management Plan

The Asbestos Hazard Emergency Response Act (AHERA) requires that schools develop and maintain an asbestos management plan that documents the recommended response actions for asbestos, note the locations of any asbestos-containing materials (ACM) on the property, and record any action taken to repair or remove the ACM. The plan must include:

- The name and address of each site with ACM and the type of ACM present
- The date of inspection
- A plan for re-inspections
- Blueprints noting locations of ACM
- A description of means to reduce ACM exposure
- A copy of any analytical results and the address of the analytical laboratory
- Contact information for a designated person responsible for the program
- A description of a communication plan for staff and students

Plans must be available for review upon demand by any staff member, parent, or labor representative.

Operations and Maintenance Program for Asbestos

For non-school businesses, operations and maintenance (O&M) programs are a means to properly manage asbestos-containing materials (ACM) in their facilities. The O&M program outlines a training program, cleaning, work practices, and surveillance to keep present ACM in good condition to reduce the risk of staff exposure. The goal is to manage ACM in place instead of developing control and abatement procedures that exceed the abilities of on-site staff.

ELEMENTS

An operations and maintenance (O&M) plan is intended to reduce the risk of exposure to asbestos by managing the materials in place instead of removing or replacing them. An O&M plan must be specific to the site and the type of asbestos found at that location. The plan should include the following:

- A training program for custodial and maintenance staff
- A notification program for all workers, occupants, and tenants as to the location of the ACM, the hazards of asbestos, and how to avoid exposure
- A routine monitoring program to assess and record any changes in the conditions of the ACM
- Administrative processes, such as permits or other work controls, to monitor activities that might disturb ACM
- Safe work practices to avoid or minimize respirable fiber generation during maintenance activities
- Records of O&M plan activities, such as control plans and inspections
- A medical surveillance and respiratory protection program to protect workers under the O&M plan

BUILDING SURVEY FOR HAZARDOUS MATERIALS PRIOR TO RENOVATION, DEMOLITION, OR OTHER CONSTRUCTION PROJECTS

Hazardous building materials (such as asbestos, lead, mercury, and PCBs) can have lasting health impacts if a worker is exposed to them during a construction or maintenance project. Asbestos fibers can be disturbed and subsequently inhaled, which can result in asbestosis or mesothelioma. Grinding lead paint can generate inhalable dusts that can cause long-term cognitive issues. Thus, a building owner must be aware of the potential presence of these materials and the impact they can have on contractors and employees.

A survey is a visual inspection of the facility to identify potential areas of concern. Once a potential material is identified, laboratory testing or another confirmation method should be conducted to confirm or refute the presence of the regulated material. Asbestos fibers are confirmed by microscope while lead requires chemical tests. If the presence of a hazardous building material is confirmed, the building owner must prepare a plan to manage the material—some materials can be managed in place (as by sealing off asbestos-containing materials for example) while others may need to be removed. Any regulated building material that is removed must be managed as a hazardous waste.

Surveys can be contracted out to environmental companies that specialize in regulated material inspections. They may also be conducted by employees with material-specific certifications.

Process and Output Based on Regulatory Framework

DETERMINING REQUIRED ENVIRONMENTAL ASSESSMENTS AND HANDLING OUTPUT FROM STUDIES

Facility owners are required to determine which regulations apply to their operations so that they may obtain the necessary operating permits and avoid penalties and fines. Under the laws for each of the major pollution categories—the Clean Air Act, the Clean Water Act, and the Resource Conservation and Recovery Act (for solid waste)—regulations describe emission limits for both specific pollutants and pollutant categories. The Environmental Protection Agency (EPA) has also established strict guidelines for the testing methods used to analyze environmental samples. Thus, the owner/operator must review the regulations, determine what pollutants must be monitored, understand what the allowable limits for release are, and implement means to monitor or test for those pollutants.

Identifying Whether Contaminant in Particular Medium Must Be Remediated

The results of **environmental sampling** are provided in the form of an analytical report to the entity that submitted the samples or requested the testing. The submitting body must then interpret the results to determine next steps, including whether remediation is required or desired levels have been achieved. Results will typically be expressed as concentration which will depend on the medium that was analyzed (soil, air, or water). Soil results may be expressed as milligram of contaminant per gram or kilogram of soil. Air results may be reported as parts per million or milligrams per liter of air. Water samples may be reported as milligrams per liter of water. The individual assessing the results must compare the analytical results to the published standards, listed in various tables in 40 CFR, to determine if additional corrective action or remediation is necessary. In some instances, the units of the analytical results must be converted to the units listed in the regulations to make a valid assessment.

Exposure Routes Based on Contamination Source

Community Exposures to Contaminated Media

Air, soil, and water can become polluted by intentional or unintentional hazardous chemical discharges. These contaminated media can then present a hazard to the surrounding communities who are exposed to them. Community chemical exposures can occur either directly or indirectly. A **direct exposure** is when a member of the public ingests, inhales, or has a dermal exposure to the contaminated media. Breathing polluted air or drinking contaminated water are both examples of direct exposure. People may also be exposed to the pollutant indirectly. In an **indirect exposure**, the individual comes into contact with something that has been contaminated by the polluted media. Indirect exposures include ingesting water while swimming in a surface water into which the groundwater discharges, eating fish that have lived in contaminated waters, or eating food that has been watered with polluted water where the plant has taken up the dissolved heavy metals.

Area of Impact of Contaminated Media

The risk of community exposure to contaminated air, water, and soil will be dependent on the media, the municipal systems, and the proximity to the release. Soil is typically confined to a specific area. Contamination will only migrate through the environment if it is carried by surface water or groundwater, including runoff. Pollutants from soil used for farming will travel as far as the food product is distributed, which has been seen in E. coli outbreaks. Polluted water will impact communities downstream from the pollutant source if those communities use the water as part of their water supply. Air emissions will impact a much larger area, including all nearby communities downwind of the release. In the cases of water and air, the level of contamination will decrease with distance from the source as the pollutant is diluted in the water or atmosphere.

Community Exposure Routes for Contaminated Groundwater

Chemical contaminants that enter underground aquifers have the potential to expose communities that rely on the water by various **exposure routes**. **Ingestion** can occur by drinking contaminated groundwater or by eating foodstuffs from farms irrigated with polluted water. A **dermal** exposure can occur by bathing or swimming in polluted water. Pollutants such as volatile organic carbons

(VOCs) have the potential to leach through the soil and collect in below-grade areas, such as basements, where they can be inhaled.

Community Exposure Routes for Contaminated Soil

Exposure to contaminated media, such as water and soil, can occur either directly or indirectly. Direct exposure can occur via inhalation of contaminated dusts, accidental ingestion (such as a child eating dirt), or contact with the polluted soil when accessing the site of the release. People can become indirectly exposed when precipitation acts as a vehicle for the chemical to reach groundwater, when edible foods planted in contaminated soil take up the pollutants, or when livestock feed on contaminated plants and their food products are subsequently consumed.

Community Exposure Routes for Air Emissions

Hazardous air pollutants (HAPs) that are not controlled and are allowed to enter the atmosphere present hazards to any community that is immediately downwind. The primary exposure route for air emissions is breathing the polluted air. The pollutant enters the body and, depending on the substance, may enter the **lower respiratory system**, where it can cause damage to the body. Some chemicals undergo atmospheric chemical reactions and, when carried by precipitation, can cause acid rain. Acid rain can result in a dermal exposure, which can have detrimental health effects in large concentrations. Other chemicals may be carried from the atmosphere to the ground, where they can pollute surface or underground municipal water sources and eventually be ingested by individuals who drink the tap water.

Health and Safety

Contaminant Routes of Exposure and Susceptible Populations

Common Routes of Entry for Chemical Exposure

An individual can be exposed to a chemical hazard by one of the four **routes of entry**—injection, ingestion, absorption, and inhalation:

- **Injection** is the subcutaneous exposure to a chemical, which allows it to bypass the protective layer of the skin. An example of an injection exposure would be a broken chemical container that pierces the skin, allowing the chemical to enter the bloodstream.
- **Ingestion** is exposure to a chemical by mouth, which causes an exposure by way of the digestive system. A person who has touched a hazardous material and then eats, drinks, applies cosmetics, takes medication, or smokes can transfer the material from their hands into their mouth, resulting in an ingestion exposure.
- **Absorption** is the movement of a chemical through the intact skin. Skin absorption can occur when certain chemicals are spilled or splashed on unprotected flesh. As the concentration of the chemical is higher on the surface of the skin then it is on the inside of the body, the chemical will move to the area of lower concentration—a process called "diffusion."
- **Inhalation** is the most common route of entry for hazardous materials. High concentrations of water-soluble chemicals can overwhelm the protection of the upper respiratory system and enter the lungs. Chemicals that are not water soluble also can bypass the protective mucosa in the upper respiratory system and pass into the lungs. Once in the lungs, chemicals can damage the lung tissue or pass into the blood through the alveoli where they can negatively impact the body.

Dose and Classes of Chemical Exposures

Although the term "**dose**" is commonly associated with pharmaceuticals, it has a broader meaning in terms of toxicology and the impacts of chemicals on the body. "Dose" relates to the amount of a chemical that the body is exposed to over the timeframe of the exposure. For example, a person standing behind the tailpipe of an older model passenger vehicle may be engulfed by a cloud of exhaust when the vehicle starts. This dose differs from that of children attending a school near a busy street. Their exposure to exhaust is much smaller in amount but also much longer—up to the number of years they will attend that school.

Doses of hazardous chemicals are often placed into one of two categories—acute or chronic. An **acute** dose is a large concentration of a chemical over a short period of time. An employee's opening of a pressurized vessel and becoming engulfed in a vapor cloud is an example of an acute exposure. Acute exposures typically result in **immediate health effects**, such as coughing, vomiting, or blisters on the skin. In most acute exposures, the health effects are short-lived. However, large exposures to toxic materials may result in death. On the other end of the spectrum is the **chronic** dose—a small concentration of chemical over a long time. Painters whose daily work involves the use of oil-based paints will be exposed to potentially hazardous petroleum distillates over their career. Chronic health effects, like tumors or cancers, show up after a generally long period of time, require extensive treatment, and may be irreversible.

Adults Susceptible to Chemical Exposures

Individual responses to a chemical exposure are based on many factors. Health, age, sex, environmental factors, and heredity all play into how an individual's body will respond to a chemical exposure. However, some groups of people are particularly susceptible to chemical exposures. The elderly are more sensitive to chemicals due to the reduced ability of their organs to metabolize chemicals, underlying health conditions, and the loss of muscle and body mass caused by aging. Females can be more sensitive to certain chemicals based on body fat percentages (lipid-soluble chemicals will reside in the body longer), overall body mass relative to males, and the fact that they bear children. Lactating women are also a high-risk group as their infants rely on them for nourishment, meaning that any chemical they may be exposed to may also be passed to the infant.

Susceptibility of Children and Developing Fetuses to Chemical Exposures

Children and fetuses are identified as high-risk groups when it comes to chemical exposures. Children are a susceptible population due to their behavior, their size, and their stage of physical development. Children spend more time on the floor or playing in the environment, and younger children especially may put random objects or materials in their mouths more than an adult would. These behaviors put them at an increased risk of exposure routes for any chemicals in their environment. Due to their small size compared to adults, a comparable chemical exposure represents a higher risk. Additionally, children **respire** at a faster rate than adults, which increases the chances and dose of an inhalation exposure. Finally, a child's body is still experiencing **organ maturation** and rapid growth. Organs may not be in a phase of development where they can properly **detoxify** the body after an exposure. A high growth rate also means that there is rapid cell reproduction, which can be impacted by chemical exposure.

Fetuses are also a susceptible population due to their rapid growth. Any chemical that interferes with or alters the development, reproduction, or specialization of cells can negatively impact the developing fetus. If the impact is severe enough, the fetus can die or may be born with defects. Additionally, fetal organ systems are in various stages of development, making them more susceptible to the impact of a chemical exposure.

Material Exposure Routes Based on Screening Thresholds

Public Health Assessment

The **Agency for Toxic Substances and Disease Registry (ATSDR)** is responsible for determining the implications of any releases of chemicals into the environment and from any hazardous waste sites, including storage and disposal facilities.

In order to identify mitigation or prevention strategies for affected communities, ATSDR has developed a process for evaluating public exposures to potential and actual environmental contamination. This process is termed a **public health assessment (PHA)**, which evaluates if a population is being, may be, or has been exposed to a chemical contaminant and what, if any, health effects are related to these exposures.

Triggers for Conducting Public Health Assessments

ATSDR and its partner agencies conduct public health assessments in the following three situations:

- A location is proposed to be placed on the **National Priority List (NPL)** of the Environmental Protection Agency (EPA), a list of Superfund cleanup sites that have known releases or have a high risk of a release.
- A petition to evaluate a site is received by ATSDR from an individual or other concerned parties.
- Another state or regulatory agency requests that ATSDR perform an assessment.

Scientific Evaluations That Comprise Public Health Assessments

When evaluating the potential impact of a release from a hazardous waste storage site, the public health assessment must evaluate multiple datasets to determine how the chemical could come into contact with people and what the effects would be. The two primary scientific evaluations are the exposure evaluation and the health effects evaluation.

- The **exposure evaluation** seeks to identify the migration of the chemical from the source to points where the community may have an exposure. An important piece of this dataset is identifying the types and amounts of chemicals at the source. This information can help to determine how the chemicals will migrate through the environment and how a person could become exposed. Air, water, and soil sampling each provide crucial data for this evaluation.
- The **health effects** evaluation is an attempt to determine the potential health effects of an exposure. If the exposure evaluation shows that people may contact the chemical, the health effects evaluation then determines what could happen. This evaluation relies on existing toxicological studies of the contaminants as well as reviews of medical and epidemiological studies.

Exposure Pathway

An **exposure pathway** is the series of events that leads from a hazardous chemical release to that chemical coming into contact with individuals in the community. It essentially traces the movement of a chemical forwards or backwards between a source and an individual, identifying how an exposure could result or how a previous exposure occurred. Exposure pathways can be used in emergency planning to prevent community exposures, or they can be used to trace an exposure to its source.

Elements

When a public health assessment is conducted, the study needs to attempt to identify who has been, is being, or could be exposed to a chemical released by a nearby facility. When analyzing a nearby population's potential exposure, the exposure pathway must be evaluated. The pathway has five elements to be considered:

- Source of the release – Where the chemical is originating from must be evaluated to determine the plume of potential exposure as well as the potential routes of exposure.
- Environmental fate and transport – The ability of the chemical to move through air, water, and soil will depend on the physical and chemical properties of the material as well as the environment of the release.
- Exposure points – Specific locations where people may come into contact with the chemical must be evaluated. For example, the exposure point for a groundwater contamination could be a water faucet whereas one for a water discharge could be a nearby river.

- Exposure route – This is the specific mode (inhalation, ingestion, absorption, etc.) by which people would contact the chemical.
- Potentially exposed populations – The evaluation must consider which nearby populations could be exposed, such as nearby schools or other sensitive populations.

Health Effects Evaluations

A health effects evaluation is one of the two scientific studies conducted for a public health assessment when evaluating the potential of community exposure to a hazardous chemical. The health effects evaluation consists of two parts—a screening analysis and an in-depth analysis. The **screening analysis** involves reviewing all the collected environmental data based on the exposure pathways. Analytical results of chemical type and concentration at community contact points are evaluated. A screening analysis of each analyte is conducted to determine next steps. If the screening analysis determines that a substance may be present in a concentration that could result in a negative health effect, then an **in-depth analysis** needs to occur. An in-depth analysis will examine only substances of concern to determine what, if any, health effects could result from an exposure.

Public Health Assessment Screening Analysis

A screening analysis is part of the health effects evaluation of a public health assessment regarding potential exposures to releases from hazardous waste facilities.

A screening analysis allows investigators to determine which substances require additional evaluations and which do not. Data collected from the analysis of environmental (air, soil, and water) samples is compared to available comparison values. A **comparison value** is a dose level that is set well below levels that have adverse health effects, thereby introducing a **safety factor** to any potential exposure. The comparison values are derived from available data and are specific to the medium (air, soil, or water) and route of exposure. If the screening analysis result is below the comparison value, the compound requires no additional analysis or consideration. For any chemical that exceeds its comparison values, an in-depth analysis is needed to determine if it poses a health risk.

Conclusions from Public Health Assessments

The goal of a public health assessment is to identify actions to prevent or eliminate public exposures to chemicals released from a location that contains hazardous waste. After conducting exposure and health effects evaluations, looking at potential exposure pathways, and evaluating environmental sample data with comparison values, the report will yield one of the following results regarding the site:

- Poses no hazard – Chemicals are properly contained, and no or little contamination is detected outside of the facility perimeter.
- Poses a hazard – Chemicals are detected at levels above their comparison values at points where the community can become exposed.
- Cannot be fully evaluated due to missing critical information – Specific data points are missing or lack sufficient validity, so a definitive decision cannot be made.

Considerations When Drawing Conclusions in Public Health Assessments

The team conducting a public health assessment will exhaustively review the exposure evaluation and the public health effects evaluation. When the investigator comes to one of the three conclusions for their report, they are to consider three factors:

- The existence of past, present, or future exposures to the chemicals at the site as well as any chemical or physical hazards – Is there a history of or a high risk of a release or exposure, and does the site exhibit other risks (fire, explosion, etc.) to the surrounding community as a direct result of materials or activities at the site?
- The susceptibility of the surrounding population – What are the demographics, age groups, facilities (e.g., schools, nursing homes), and other compounding factors (e.g., poor air quality) that may contribute to the risk of exposure or the degree of health effects if any exposure is experienced?
- The likelihood of an exposure that can result in a negative health effect – What is the estimated probability of an exposure, given an evaluation of the amount of materials, the immediate environment (i.e., rivers, aquifers, topography, etc.), proximity to the nearby population, and the sizes of any proximal towns or cities?

Job Hazard Analysis

Job Hazard Analysis

A hazard is the inherent property of a material or process to cause harm to an employee. If the hazard is not controlled, then the likelihood of injury or illness increases.

A **job hazard analysis (JHA)** is a systematic approach to identifying the hazards of a job or task and identifying ways to control the hazard to prevent injury or illness. Eliminating or reducing the hazards lowers the risk of employees being injured while they execute their jobs, improving output and reducing costs.

Identifying Jobs or Tasks That Would Benefit from Job Hazard Analysis

Conducting a proper and actionable job hazard analysis (JHA) requires time and energy. Production could be impacted as employee resources need to be diverted to produce meaningful results. Additionally, not all jobs may benefit from such a process. Thus, it is important for the organization to identify and prioritize jobs or tasks that should be undergo a JHA. Jobs and tasks that may be selected include the following:

- Jobs that have a high injury rate as reflected in injury or illness logs
- Jobs that result in or could result in severe injuries (such as those that lead to death or amputations), injuries multiple workers, or injuries that require a long time off work
- Tasks where a simple human error could result in a severe injury or death
- New jobs, or changes to a process that could lead to errors or mistakes that result in injury
- Complex tasks that have multiple steps, where the risk of injury depends on order of operations or where written instructions are required
- Jobs or tasks that are not performed very often and have a potential for injury

Steps of Job Hazard Analysis

A job hazard analysis is used to identify and proactively correct potential sources of injury and inefficiency in a job or task.

First, the job or task to be analyzed must be identified.

Next, the job is broken down into sequential steps. This is typically done by observing a seasoned employee performing the job or task and by then writing down the steps they execute to perform the action.

Next, each step is evaluated for potential hazards and potential causes of incidents. For example, the first step in using a portable ladder is to inspect the equipment. If the equipment is not properly inspected, hazards such as broken rails, splinters, or cracked steps may be missed, which could result in a fall.

The final step in a hazard analysis is to develop solutions for all identified hazards. The hazards must be removed or reduced to make the job safer and to decrease the risk of injury. Hazard controls may be prioritized and implemented based on cost or effectiveness.

Components of Hazard Scenario

After the job to be evaluated has been identified and broken down into discrete steps, the hazards of each step need to be identified. Organizations should seek a consistent method of identifying potential hazards associated with a task. By constructing a **hazard scenario** for each task using the same components, the hazard identification process will be standardized. Components of a hazard scenario can include the following:

- Environment – where the job is occurring, and whether that environment involves any risks to the employee
- Exposure – who is exposed to the hazard, how many people are exposed, and how often they are exposed to the hazard
- **Trigger** – what immediate actions, conditions, or decisions might lead to the hazard causing an injury
- **Consequence** – what type of injury or illness would result, how sever would it be, and how many people would be injured or exposed
- **Contributing factors** – any other relevant factors

Hazard Controls

Hazard controls are methods implemented to reduce the degree of the hazard or its impact on an employee who is exposed to it. Hazards that are identified in a job hazard analysis must have controls implemented for the process to be successful. Hazard controls fall into one of three categories:

- **Engineering controls** – control measures that eliminate, enclose, isolate, or otherwise remove the hazard (e.g., machine guards, exhaust ventilation)
- **Administrative controls** – processes or procedures to reduce an employee's exposure to the hazard (e.g., warning signs, standard operating procedures, limiting time of exposure, alarm systems)
- **Personal protective equipment** – items worn by employees to reduce hazard exposure (e.g., earplugs, cut-resistant gloves, respirators)

Application of Hazard Control Hierarchy in Job Hazard Analysis

The **National Institute of Occupational Safety and Health (NIOSH)** has established a **hierarchy of controls** to assist organizations in selecting proper hazard controls. When selecting a control measure for an identified hazard, the safety professional should identify potential engineering controls first, followed by administrative controls, and finally, as a last resort, personal protective equipment (PPE).

Engineering controls are the preferred method as they directly eliminate, remove, or reduce the hazard. A local exhaust ventilation system directs hazardous fumes away from a worker, thereby eliminating the exposure, while a general ventilation system reduces concentrations of fumes in the air.

Administrative controls are dependent on human behavior to be effective. If warning signs or signals are ignored or standard operating procedures (SOPs) are not followed, then protection offered by these controls is minimal or nonexistent. PPE is the least preferred method as this control simply places a barrier between the employee and the hazard. No mitigation of the hazard has occurred, and any failure of the equipment or any failure of the employee to properly don or use the equipment will result in an exposure to the hazard. PPE is often used as a last resort or as a temporary control while engineering controls are being installed.

Review Video: Risk Management and Hazard Control
Visit mometrix.com/academy and enter code: 625808

Process Safety Management

Process Safety Management

Businesses that use **highly hazardous chemicals (HHC)** are at a higher risk of explosions, fires, large-scale releases, and other major incidents. Due to the risks these facilities face, the Occupational Safety and Health Administration (OSHA) has promulgated a **process safety management** standard. The intent of process safety management is to increase the safety at facilities that fall under requirements as well as to protect the equipment and the facility. Developed by reviewing past accidents involving HHC, the standard works using the concept that various activities at a facility are interrelated when it comes to health and safety. By considering how all the activities and processes at a site are connected and how they can impact one another, the employer can improve the overall safety of the site.

Process Safety Management Program

Implementation Requirements

Any business that uses, handles, stores, or otherwise manages highly hazardous chemicals (HHC) above their threshold quantities must implement a process safety management program. Additionally, specific industries have developed **process safety guidance**, as in the cases of petrochemical companies, chemical manufacturers, and pyrotechnic manufacturers. Under the Occupational Safety and Health Administration (OSHA) standard, any facility that meets any of the criteria below is subject to the process safety management standard:

- Has HHCs listed in Appendix A at quantities above the listed thresholds
- Has processes that involve more than 10,000 pounds of a Class 1 flammable gas
- Stores petroleum fuels for on-site consumption, such as propane tanks for forklifts or refueling tanks for gasoline-powered vehicles
- Stores flammable liquids with a flash point less than 100 degrees Fahrenheit in atmospheric tanks that are not chilled or otherwise refrigerated

Components

A compliant **process safety management (PSM)** program is a comprehensive evaluation of the risks and risk mitigation strategies in facilities that have a potential for a catastrophic chemical incident. The program has fourteen elements that must be considered:

- Compliance audits
- Training
- Contractors
- Hot work
- Process safety information
- Process hazard analysis
- Mechanical integrity
- Operating procedures
- Incident investigation
- Change management
- Employee participation
- Trade secrets
- Pre-startup safety review
- Emergency planning and response

Data Considered in Compilation of PSI Compilation

During the process safety management (PSM) process, the employer must compile data on the chemicals that trigger the standard. This data, **process safety information (PSI)**, is critical to the overall effectiveness of the PSM program. PSI includes the following:

- Toxicity data
- Exposure limits
- Physical data
- Reactivity data
- Corrosivity data
- Stability data
- Effects of mixing with other substances

Most of this required information, which must be written into the PSM program, can be located on the safety data sheet for the material.

Process Flow Diagrams

A critical component of process safety management (PSM) is to understand how highly hazardous chemicals (HHCs) move through the facility and what other hazards and chemicals these HHCs may be involved in. To facilitate this understanding, a facility must construct a **process flow diagram (PFD)**. A PFD is a block diagram that visually presents the major process equipment and any connections to other equipment. In addition to the equipment involved, a PFD may include flow rates, temperatures, pressures, and other relevant conditions where a deviation could result in a release.

Equipment Information Included in PSM Program

As part of the process safety management (PSM) program, the employer must compile information related to the equipment that contains, transfers, or otherwise comes into contact with highly hazardous chemicals. Required information includes the following:

- Piping and instrument diagrams (P&IDs)
- Materials used in equipment construction
- Electrical classification
- Relief system design and triggers
- Ventilation system design
- Safety systems
- Material and energy balances (for systems built after 1992)

Employers must also have documentation showing that all related equipment complies with **recognized and generally accepted good engineering practices (RAGAGEP)**.

Process Hazard Analysis

One of the required elements of a process safety management (PSM) program is a **process hazard analysis (PHA)**. The PHA is a systematic identification and evaluation of potential causes of fires, explosions, or releases of highly hazardous chemicals. In addition to these potential causes, the PHA also considers the consequences of those events, including **immediate impacts** (affecting the facility) and **external impacts** (affecting the surrounding community). Risks identified in the PHA must also identify safeguards to reduce the risk as much as possible.

Training Required Under PSM Program

The Occupational Safety and Health Administration (OSHA) puts an emphasis on effective employee training in hazards, hazard mitigation, and emergency response. Under the process safety management (PSM) standard, employee training is required for all employees who work with processes involving highly hazardous chemicals.

Training must address process-specific safety and health hazards, operating procedures, emergency shutdown processes, and safe practices. Employers must provide initial and refresher training under the standard.

Mechanical Integrity Requirements for PSM Program

The **mechanical integrity** element of a process safety management (PSM) program requires that the equipment involved with highly hazardous chemicals must be kept in good working order to avoid conditions that could lead to an incident. Equipment must be appropriately designed, tested, inspected, repaired, and maintained.

Site Safety Plan Components

Activities Under Scope of HAZWOPER Standard

Working with hazardous materials puts employees at a high risk of chemical exposure. Activities involving hazardous waste are of particular concern as the materials may be mixtures of chemicals that present multiple hazards, may not be in original packaging, may be in containers that are compromised, or may have spilled into water or soil. Due to the risk, the Occupational Safety and Health Administration (OSHA) has promulgated the **hazardous waste operations and emergency response (HAZWOPER)** standard to outline protective measures (such as air monitoring), designate training, and decrease the health risks to employees. The following groups of employees must be HAZWOPER trained:

- Employees who participate in cleanup operations of hazardous waste sites
- Employees who participate in corrective actions for hazardous waste storage sites that have detected releases that must be mitigated under the Resource Conservation and Recovery Act (RCRA)
- Employees who work at a treatment, storage, and disposal facility (TSDF) that manages hazardous waste
- Employees who respond to chemical spills or releases in any capacity

Application of Site Safety Plan Under HAZWOPER Standard

The hazardous waste operations and emergency response (HAZWOPER) standard requires that an employer conducting cleanup or emergency response actions prepare a **site safety plan (SSP)**, sometimes referred to as a "health and safety plan (HSAP)." The SSP is specific to the location and the operations being conducted. It outlines how the employer will identify hazards, how the employer will select and use personal protective equipment, and what training is required for employees at the site.

Elements of Site Safety Plan

Site safety plans (SSPs) under the hazardous waste operations and emergency response (HAZWOPER) standard are intended to identify hazards specific to the location, communicate those hazards to employees, and establish controls to protect employees from the identified hazards. An SSP must contain the following elements:

- A hazard or risk analysis for each task being conducted to identify and quantify the hazards employees may encounter
- Employee training assignments to make sure that employees have received proper training for the tasks they will be conducting
- Required personal protective equipment
- Medical surveillance requirements for employees working on site
- An air monitoring program that includes the frequency and type of monitoring or sampling, the instrumentation used, and maintenance and calibration schedules
- Site control measures to keep unauthorized personnel out of hazardous areas
- Decontamination procedures
- An emergency response plan
- Confined space entry procedures
- A spill containment program.

Updating Site Safety Plans

A site safety plan (SSP) must be updated when conditions change (e.g., a change in the weather), when additional hazards are identified (e.g., finding a previously unknown rusty drum containing an unknown liquid), or when the operation at the site enters a different phase (e.g., pivoting from emergency response to cleanup).

Emergency Response Plan Elements

Chemical Spill ERP

The Occupational Safety and Health Administration (OSGA) outlines the requirements for emergency response plan (ERPs) that address the risk of chemical releases and spills. Such a plan must include pre-emergency planning and coordination with outside response agencies, including which contractors will be used for cleanup and which public agencies need to be notified. The ERP must describe the roles of responders, the chain of command, and how the responders will communicate through their chain of command. The plan must describe how employees can recognize a potential spill and what controls can be used to prevent or contain releases. Regarding large releases, the ERP should identify safe distances and places of refuge to allow for evacuation of the site and accounting for all evacuees. The ERP must describe how nonessential personnel will be kept out of the danger area if there is a spill and how the danger area will be identified. The plan must describe the personal protective equipment available to the spill response team and any other emergency equipment available to them. Evacuation routes and emergency medical procedures must also be included. Finally, decontamination procedures and a "lessons learned" critique are required elements for any ERP.

Hazardous Material Containment

Spill Containment Plan

Activities that are covered by the hazardous waste operations and emergency response (HAZWOPER) standard, including cleanup at hazardous waste sites and emergency response to releases, must have a spill containment plan as part of their site safety plan. The spill containment plan is a preventative plan for when operations may result in a major spill or release. The measures identified must be capable of containing the entire volume of material that may be released.

Spill Containment Strategies

If there is a risk of a spill that would expose employees to a hazardous chemical, the employer must develop a spill containment program to contain and control such a spill. Classic strategies include building dikes or digging ditches to capture and direct spilled fluids. The application of absorbent materials has also been a traditional method of stopping the movement of a fluid during a spill or in the cleanup of a spill.

Advancements in technology have resulted in a broader array of spill containment strategies. **Pressurized absorbent** contained in a fire extinguisher-like apparatus allows for a quick response to a spill. **Solidifying agents** work as double-action agents—if applied to the edges of the spill first, they act as a berm, stopping the flow, and can then be applied to the rest of the material, allowing it to be removed. Acid and base **neutralizers** as well as **activated carbon** can not only absorb the liquid but also reduce or eliminate the hazard of the substance they are applied to.

Benefits of Proper Hazardous Material Containment

Containment is defined as the action of keeping something that is harmful under control or within established limits. When applied to hazardous materials, it means to preventing the spread of a chemical into the environment or close to employees, either of which could lead to exposures. Proper containment of hazardous chemicals prevents the chemicals from migrating through the environment as this requires an expensive cleanup operation. Protecting employees from exposures reduces injuries, lost time, employee turnover, and workers' compensation losses.

Containment can range from simply inspecting containers for leaks or damage to the installation of double-wall storage tanks and leak detection systems.

Secondary Containment Requirements for Tanks Containing Hazardous Materials or Hazardous Waste

A **tank** is any stationary, non-earthen device that stores liquid hazardous chemicals (either waste or materials that will be used in production). Because of the volume of material typically stored in tanks, measures must be taken to prevent and detect any releases into the environment.

The Environmental Protection Agency (EPA) requires that tanks have **secondary containment** systems—protections that are additional to the primary container and that should have the following characteristics:

- Constructed of materials that are compatible with the chemicals contained in the primary tank and that can withstand the environmental conditions as well as contact with the material in the tank
- Situated on a foundation that can support the primary and secondary system and is not impacted by settling, compression, or uplift of the soil
- Equipped with a leak detection system for both the primary and secondary containment systems that will actuate within 24 hours of a release
- Designed to remove spilled or leaked materials as well as precipitation, as by sloping or by a drainage system that is emptied within 24 hours of a leak or rain event

Active and Passive Containment Systems

The Environmental Protection Agency (EPA) uses the terms "active containment system" and "passive containment system" to describe facilities that use and store oil. An **active containment system** requires personnel to deploy the system or operate the system. An example of an active system is a spill kit, where the employee must respond and apply the absorbent materials. **Passive containment systems** are installed before leaks occur and do not require human intervention. Drip pads, berms, and drains are examples of passive systems.

Containers

The Environmental Protection Agency (EPA) provides a definition for containers that may store hazardous waste or materials that distinguishes them from tanks. Containers, under this definition, are portable and can be used to store, transport, treat, act as a permanent disposal container for, or otherwise handle a material. The material within can be either a liquid or a solid.

Requirements for Containers Used to Store or Otherwise Transport Hazardous Waste

Containers used to hold hazardous waste are regulated by the Environmental Protection Agency (EPA). The integrity of the container is critical in keeping the material from leaking into the environment. Therefore, the following requirements exist for hazardous waste containers:

- They must be compatible with the waste they are intended to hold (e.g., no metal drums for corrosive wastes).
- They must have an affixed lid that is in place whenever material is not being added to or removed from the container.
- They must be inspected on a weekly basis for leaks, rust, or other signs of impending failure.

Product Labeling Requirements

LABELING REQUIREMENTS

The Hazard Communication Standard delineates how a product manufacturer or producer conveys the hazards of substances to those who work with the substances. One of the principal ways of conveying this information is appropriate labeling. According to the Globally Harmonized System (GHS) of Classification and Labelling of Chemicals, as referenced in the Hazard Communication Standard, a proper label must contain the following information:

- Product identifier – the name of the material, which may include the scientific name, the common name, and other synonyms that identify the material
- Signal word – either "Warning" or "Hazard," with "Warning" indicating less severity than "Hazard"
- Hazard statements – standardized phrases describing the nature and severity of a chemical hazard; corresponding numeric codes
- Pictograms – one of nine graphics that nonverbally convey the hazard class or classes of the material
- Precautionary statements – standardized phrases that describe methods of minimizing or preventing exposure to the material; corresponding numeric codes
- Contact information – the name, address, and telephone number of the manufacturer, importer, or producer

Practice Test

Want to take this practice test in an online interactive format?
Check out the bonus page, which includes interactive practice questions and much more: **mometrix.com/bonus948/chmm**

1. Butane is

a. a carboxylic acid with 1 carbon atom.
b. an alcohol with 2 carbon atoms.
c. an aldehyde with 3 carbon atoms.
d. an alkane with 4 carbon atoms.

2. The flashpoint of a substance is

a. the temperature at which a liquid will begin to evaporate and form a gas.
b. the temperature at which a liquid will begin to produce a sufficient amount of vapor to cause a fire if there is both an ignition source and air present.
c. the temperature at which a solid will begin to liquefy.
d. the temperature at which a substance will cause a fire without an ignition source if there is air present.

3. According to the Environmental Protection Agency (EPA), a substance should be considered a delayed health hazard if the substance may

a. cause an individual to experience an adverse effect after the individual has been exposed to the substance for a long period of time.
b. cause an individual to experience an adverse effect after the individual has been exposed to the substance for a short period of time.
c. cause a potentially dangerous chemical reaction after it is exposed to another substance such as air or water.
d. cause a fire to occur, cause a fire to burn longer, or cause a fire to burn more violently than it would typically be able to burn without the substance.

4. The US Department of Transportation (DOT) defines a combustible substance as

a. a substance with a flashpoint of no more than 60°C or 140°F.
b. a substance with a flashpoint of more than 60°C or 140°F, but less than 93°C or 200°F.
c. a mixture that contains a substance with a flashpoint of more than 60°C or 140°F that has been mixed with a substance with a flashpoint of less than 60°C or 140°F when the mixture is transported at a temperature less than the flashpoint of both substances.
d. a substance with a flashpoint of more than 93°C or 200°F.

5. Determine the volume of 0.5M sodium bicarbonate ($NaHCO_3$) that an individual would need to neutralize 1 L of 0.1M phosphoric acid (H_3PO_4).

a. 0.2 mL
b. 50 mL
c. 200 mL
d. 600 mL

6. A pressure of 3 bars is equal to approximately

a. 2.2128 foot-pounds.
b. 14.5 pounds of force/square inch.
c. 25.0359 pounds.
d. 43.5 pounds of force/square inch.

7. What is systemic sampling?

a. A sample collection strategy in which an individual determines the locations from which he or she will collect samples by using a program or table that lists the locations at random
b. A sample collection strategy in which an individual determines the locations from which he or she will collect samples by using a system that identifies specific locations throughout the area where the individual can collect samples from on a regular basis
c. A sample collection strategy in which an individual determines the locations from which he or she will collect samples based on information about the areas that have been contaminated in the past and the areas that now appear to be contaminated
d. A sample collection strategy in which an individual collects samples from convenient locations without any apparent system

8. What is a sampling plan?

a. A series of objectives and procedures that an individual or an organization can use to ensure that all of the samples that the individual or organization collects are collected and analyzed properly
b. The objectives that the individual or organization attempts to achieve by collecting samples
c. The amount of reliability that the individual or organization realistically hopes to achieve in regards to the information that the individual or organization collects
d. The reports that the individual or organization intends to generate from the information that the individual or organization collects

9. The amount of a substance that an individual must be exposed to in a single dose for that exposure to prove fatal at least 50% of the time is known as the

a. threshold dose.
b. median effective dose.
c. median lethal concentration.
d. median lethal dose.

10. A risk assessment procedure in which an individual or an organization attempts to examine the different ways that an individual may be exposed to a substance is known as

a. a dose-response assessment.
b. an exposure assessment.
c. hazard identification.
d. risk characterization.

11. The Environmental Protection Agency (EPA) requires a Risk Management Plan (RMP) to include all of the following elements EXCEPT:

a. An executive summary that provides information about the hazardous substances that the organization handles.
b. The procedures and policies that the organization plans to use to prevent emergencies and improve safety.
c. The worst-case scenarios for each of the different ways that the organization uses a hazardous substance.
d. A summary of all risk management data that the organization has collected from risk assessments during the past five years.

12. A Risk Management Plan (RMP) analysis in which an organization attempts to create a series of procedures that a facility can use to respond to the release of a hazardous substance for a situation in which the hazardous substance does NOT spread as far as possible is known as

a. an alternative release scenario analysis.
b. an offsite consequence analysis.
c. a process hazard analysis.
d. a worst-case scenario analysis.

13. Determine the hazard quotient for an animal that will be exposed to 5.0 mg/kg of chromium per day if the maximum dose that the animal may receive per day is 2.5 mg/kg.

a. 0.5
b. 2
c. 5
d. 12.5

14. The Occupational Safety and Health Administration (OSHA) requires a safety data sheet (SDS, formerly MSDS) to include all of the following information EXCEPT:

a. The name of the substance, the name of the organization that prepared the MSDS, contact information for the organization that prepared the MSDS, and the date on which the MSDS was prepared.
b. The ingredients included in the substance, the characteristics of the substance, the dangers that the substance poses, the different ways that an individual may be exposed to the substance, the chemicals that the substance may react with, and the conditions that may cause the substance to ignite or explode.
c. The procedures that an individual should use to protect him or herself from the substance, the procedures that an individual should follow if the individual is exposed to more of the substance than is typically considered safe, and the equipment that the individual should use while handling the substance.
d. The procedures that the employer will use to minimize the impact that the substance has on individuals both inside and outside the facility if the employer is unable to contain the substance's release.

15. The Environmental Protection Agency (EPA) may require a facility to obtain a Resource Conservation and Recovery Act (RCRA) Permit if

a. the facility is a small-quantity generator (SQG) which stores hazardous waste on-site for a period longer than 180 days, but less than 270 days as long as that waste is transported to a treatment facility within 200 miles of the facility generating the waste.
b. the facility stores hazardous waste in an off-site location that is near the facility, operated by the facility, able to house the waste appropriately, and does not store more waste than it is legally allowed to store.
c. the facility stores hazardous waste on-site so that the waste may be treated in the appropriate container or tank.
d. the facility is a large quantity generator (LQG) which stores hazardous waste on-site for a period of no more than 90 days.

16. The US Department of Transportation (DOT) requires an individual transporting a hazardous material to

a. obtain a manifest that describes the type of hazardous material and the amount of hazardous material that the individual is transporting if the individual is transporting that material to an accumulation site next to the facility via a public road.
b. ensure that the container in which the hazardous material is transported has the appropriate DOT labels and placards, that the facility which generated the material has provided a manifest describing the type of material and the amount of material that the individual is transporting, and that all of the material reaches its intended destination.
c. ensure that the facility which generated the material has the appropriate RCRA permits to store the material until it can be transported and that the facility has Safety Data Sheets (SDS) for each substance that needs to be transported.
d. obtain a signed document which indicates that the facility that generated the material will be required to clean up the material in the event of a spill.

17. According to the U.S Department of Transportation, a corrosive liquid should be classified as a

a. Class 2 Hazard.
b. Class 4 Hazard.
c. Class 6 Hazard.
d. Class 8 Hazard.

18. The Resource Conservation and Recovery Act's (RCRA's) derived-from rule states that

a. an area of soil or water that contains hazardous waste should be considered hazardous if the soil or water has at least one hazardous characteristic.
b. any substance that is a mixture of hazardous and nonhazardous substances should be considered hazardous as long as the substance has at least one hazardous characteristic.
c. any substance that is created as a by-product of a process involving a hazardous waste should be considered hazardous if the waste itself is listed.
d. any substance that is created as a by-product of an industrial process, the disposal of a toxic substance, or a toxic spill should be considered hazardous if it is included on the Environmental Protection Agency's (EPA's) list of hazardous substances.

19. A hospital is attempting to determine the appropriate way to dispose of a piece of medical equipment that has been classified as a Class A low-level radioactive waste, but only has a half life of approximately three days. The hospital is required to

a. isolate the equipment until the radioactive atoms completely decay and then trash it.
b. bury the equipment so that it is no less than five meters from the surface until the radioactive atoms completely decay.
c. turn the equipment over to a low-level radioactive waste disposal facility.
d. isolate the equipment in a pool of water in a secure, contained space until the radioactive atoms completely decay.

20. What is source reduction?

a. Any procedure or action that allows a facility to reduce the amount of solid or hazardous waste that it would typically produce
b. Any procedure or action that allows a facility to convert hazardous waste into something that a consumer can use
c. Any procedure or action that allows a facility to manage less waste than it would typically be required to manage
d. Any procedure or action outside the recycling or treatment process that allows a facility to release less pollution or hazardous waste into the environment or the waste stream than it would typically release

21. Which of the following procedures is typically an important part of the recycling process?

a. Any process and/or equipment modification that causes an unused substance to produce less pollution than it would typically produce
b. Waste segregation
c. Inventory control
d. Raw material substitution

22. A facility that has accidently released a hazardous substance into a nearby river is attempting to determine how far the substance will be able to spread. Determine the distance that the substance will travel in eight hours if the contaminant is traveling at the same rate as the water in the river and the water is flowing at an average rate of approximately 1.25 m/s

a. 10 km
b. 36 km
c. 60 km
d. 100 km

23. All of the following environmental characteristics may indicate that a hazardous substance has caused an ecosystem impact EXCEPT:

a. A change in the way that the animals behave or a change in the way that the animals interact with the environment.
b. An increase in the number of animals belonging to a particular species within a particular area.
c. A sample which indicates that a hazardous substance has been released into the environment.
d. A decrease in the number of animals belonging to a particular species within a particular area.

24. An emergency plan describing the procedures that a facility will follow to eliminate or reduce the impact that a hazardous substance may have on individuals outside the facility and/or the impact that the substance may have on the environment if an accidental release occurs is known as

a. an RCRA contingency plan.
b. a SARA community response plan.
c. a HAZWOPER plan.
d. a HazCom plan.

25. The DECIDE process consists of six steps. The correct sequence for these steps is:

a. Do, Evaluate, Choose, Identify, Detect, Estimate
b. Detect, Estimate, Choose, Identify, Do, Evaluate
c. Detect, Evaluate, Choose, Identify, Do, Estimate
d. Do, Eliminate, Classify, Isolate, Detect, Evaluate

26. A treatment method in which bacteria that requires oxygen to survive is used to break down a hazardous organic substance is known as

a. an aerobic treatment system.
b. an anaerobic treatment system.
c. stabilization.
d. solidification.

27. A Primary NAAQS is

a. a standard established by the Environmental Protection Agency (EPA) that is designed to limit the amount of a specific pollutant that can be released into the air to reduce the impact that that particular pollutant has on the environment and the welfare of individuals living in that environment.
b. a standard established by the Environmental Protection Agency (EPA) that is designed to limit the amount of a specific pollutant that can be released into the air to reduce the impact that that particular pollutant has on the health of individuals living in the polluted area.
c. a standard established by the Clean Air Act that requires a facility to keep the amount of hazardous air pollutants (HAPS) that the facility produces as low as reasonably possible.
d. a standard established by the Clear Air Act that requires an organization to assess the effect that a new facility will have on the air quality of the area in which the new facility will be built before it is built.

28. What is a Transaction Screening?

a. A site assessment in which an environmental professional interviews anyone who may have information about the site including site managers and local officials, examines any and all applicable records, inspects the site, and issues a report that indicates whether additional assessments are required or not
b. A site assessment in which a representative of the organization interviews the individuals who own the site, interviews the individuals who use the site, examines government records, examines historic land-use documents, and conducts a brief site visit to determine if additional assessments are required
c. A site assessment in which an environmental professional collects samples, analyzes samples, and issues a report which indicates the findings of the analysis and the appropriate course of action
d. A site assessment in which an environmental professional collects and analyzes samples to determine if the contaminants that were identified in other site assessments have been removed and/or are now within acceptable levels

29. A remediation method in which a section of contaminated soil is removed, heated to a high temperature, and returned to the same general area is known as

a. a thermal soil treatment.
b. soil excavation.
c. soil vapor extraction.
d. biopile treatment.

30. There is evidence to indicate that PCBs may have a significant environmental impact because they can

a. damage the ozone layer.
b. exist naturally in the environment, but may also be found in many homes and buildings.
c. be used to build pipes and, as a result, may contaminate drinking water.
d. build up in the soil near a body of water and contaminate fish living in that water.

31. What is the most likely route of entry for a hazardous chemical in the workplace?

a. Absorption
b. Ingestion
c. Inhalation
d. Injection

32. The Occupational Safety and Health Administration's (OSHA's) Permit-Required Confined Space standard requires a facility to obtain a permit and take special steps to minimize the risk to an employee if the confined space

a. may contain a hazardous substance that can trap, injure, or kill the individual.
b. has enough room that an employee can enter the space and work.
c. is not intended for continuous use.
d. can only be entered or exited from a small number of locations which makes it difficult for an employee to leave the space quickly.

33. A radiation protection program should include all of the following elements EXCEPT:

a. A radiation safety officer, a radiation safety committee, or a radiation safety organization depending on the size of the facility and the size of the organization running the facility
b. Documents which prove that the facility is authorized to handle radioactive materials, records of accidents, records of the onsite radiation levels, records that indicate the amount of radioactive material currently on the premises, and records that can be used to track the radioactive materials and the individuals that might have been exposed to those materials as they moved throughout the facility
c. A document that describes the amount of radioactive substance that the organization expects to handle on an annual basis and a statement that indicates that the owner of the facility certifies that the information in the document is accurate
d. Procedures that employees should follow while handling radioactive materials, procedures for assessing the effectiveness of the program, procedures to identify and correct leaks or other problems within the facility that may expose an individual or the environment to more radioactive material than is absolutely necessary, and the procedures that the facility should follow in the event of an emergency

34. The ALARA principle suggests that all of the following techniques are effective ways to reduce the risk that an individual will experience an adverse effect from radiation EXCEPT:

a. Limit the amount of time that an individual is exposed to a radioactive substance
b. Establish procedures to ensure that the individual's exposure to a radioactive substance never exceeds the legal limits established by the Nuclear Regulatory Commission
c. Remove as much of the radioactive substance as possible from an individual's skin and body if the individual is exposed
d. Contain the radioactive substance and use protective equipment to prevent the substance from escaping and/or entering the body of an individual working near it

35. Studies have shown that exposure to asbestos may cause

a. anemia, brain damage, chronic stomach pain, hearing loss, kidney cancer, kidney damage, and other similar adverse effects.
b. bone damage, hair loss, a significant decrease in an individual's white blood cell count, skin cancer, and other similar adverse effects.
c. an increase in the amount of fluid or plaque present in the lungs, lung cancer, mesothelioma, warts, and other similar adverse effects.
d. chloracne, hair loss, liver cancer, liver damage, skin irritation, weight loss, and other similar adverse effects.

36. According to the Environmental Protection Agency (EPA), a facility may assume that a piece of oil-filled electrical equipment is non-PCB for the purposes of the Toxic Substance Control Act if

a. the equipment was manufactured after July 2, 1979, and the facility is attempting to dispose of the equipment.
b. the equipment was manufactured after July 2, 1979, and it is currently in storage.
c. the equipment has leaked or spilled a chemical substance, but was manufactured after July 2, 1979.
d. the equipment was manufactured after July 2, 1979, and is currently in use.

37. The Resource Conservation and Recovery Act (RCRA) is

a. a federal statute that grants the Environmental Protection Agency (EPA) the ability to identify the individuals that are responsible for the hazardous release of a substance, the ability to compel the individuals responsible to clean-up the release even if the individuals are no longer using the site, and the ability to fund clean-up operations if it is impossible to identify and/or compel the individuals who are responsible.
b. a federal statute that grants the EPA the ability to establish hazardous waste regulations so that they can monitor and control hazardous waste throughout the waste stream.
c. a federal statute that requires oil facilities to have plans in place to prevent, fund, and clean-up oil spills.
d. a federal statute that is designed to encourage each facility to reduce the amount of pollution that the facility generates by requiring the facility to disclose to the public information about the amount of pollution that the facility creates.

38. According to the Clean Air Act, a facility will be required to use the Best Available Control Technology Standard if

a. the facility produces hazardous air pollutants.
b. the facility is already located in an area in which the level of criteria pollutants in the air exceeds the limit established by the Environmental Protection Agency (EPA), but the controls that would typically be installed may not be practical.
c. the facility is located in an area in which the level of criteria pollutants in the air exceeds the limit established by the EPA and the facility has just begun to produce a criteria pollutant.
d. the facility is located in an area in which the level of criteria pollutants in the air does not exceed the limit established by the EPA, and the facility has just begun to produce a criteria pollutant.

39. What is the penalty for a knowing violation of the Resource Conservation and Recovery Act?

a. A civil penalty of no more than $27,500 per day and/or a criminal penalty of no more than one year in prison
b. A civil penalty of no more than $27,500 per day and/or a criminal penalty of no more than five years in prison
c. A civil penalty of no more than $50,000 per day and/or a criminal penalty of at least 2 years, but no more than 5 years in prison
d. A civil penalty of no more than $1,000,000 per day and/or a criminal penalty of no more than 15 years in prison

40. The Occupational Safety and Health (OSH) Act's Lockout/Tagout Standard requires an employer to

a. install emergency control systems and/or implement emergency procedures that will allow the employer to limit the amount of airborne toxins to which an employee will be exposed.
b. provide employees with equipment that will limit the amount of lead to which the employee will be exposed.
c. install a device in any machine that may expose an employee to electricity, a hazardous chemical, or another hazardous substance that will prevent the machine from automatically starting when an employee is near it.
d. provide employees with information about the hazards that they may be exposed to, the procedures that employees should use to reduce the risk of injury from these hazards, and the actions that the employer and employees are expected to take in the event of an accident.

41. A train carrying mixed waste from a nuclear power plant would be regulated by the

a. US Department of Transportation (DOT), the Environmental Protection Agency (EPA), the Nuclear Regulatory Commission (NRC), and the Department of Energy (DOE).
b. US Department of Transportation, the US Department of Defense (DOD), and the US Department of Energy.
c. US Department of Transportation, the US Department of Energy, and the Nuclear Regulatory Commission.
d. US Department of Transportation and the Environmental Protection Agency.

42. What is the IARC?

a. An international organization that studies a variety of chemical substances to identify substances that may cause or increase an individual's risk of cancer
b. An international organization that establishes standards designed to ensure that a variety of different industries are able to use a series of uniform procedures, methods, and data formats
c. An international organization that establishes standards and international regulations for the transport of dangerous goods by sea to ensure that hazardous cargo is transported in a safe and responsible manner
d. An international organization that establishes standards and international regulations for the transport of dangerous goods by air to ensure that hazardous materials can be transported in a safe and responsible manner

43. A facility is required to make a report to the Environmental Protection Agency (EPA) for

a. any event that causes more than $50,000 in property damage or any event in which an individual is killed, in which an individual is hospitalized, in which public areas or private homes and businesses may need to be evacuated, and any event in which the operation of an aircraft or the operation of any major mode of transportation may be significantly hindered or become impossible.
b. any event in which an employee is killed and/or at least three employees are hospitalized.
c. any event in which a facility releases a radioactive substance, in which a facility may release a radioactive substance, or in which a fire breaks out in a facility containing a radioactive substance.
d. any event in which a facility releases a hazardous substance into the environment in excess of the reportable quantity (RQ) established for that substance.

44. All of the following methods are effective ways for a Certified Hazardous Materials Manager (CHMM) to reduce the economic impact that the production, use, storage, or disposal of a hazardous substance may have on a facility EXCEPT:

a. Checking the facility's permits and reports to make sure that the facility has the appropriate permits, is filing the appropriate reports, and that the facility does not have any problems that need to be addressed.
b. Examining the way that substances are used within the facility and the purpose of each substance in the facility to determine if there are suitable alternatives.
c. Reducing the amount of training that each of the individuals within the facility receives, so that each individual is only taught the basic skills that he/she needs for his/ her position.
d. Consulting employees, experts, and other individuals within the industry to identify new methods and techniques.

45. What is the first thing that a facility's security team should do during an emergency in which a hazardous substance has been released?

a. Check the emergency plan to identify the appropriate procedures and the appropriate course of action
b. Identify the best way to evacuate the building and help with the evacuation
c. Secure the site and wait for emergency personnel
d. Call for help

46. The Occupational Safety and Health Administration's (OSHA's) Process Safety Management Standard requires a facility to do all of the following EXCEPT:

a. Begin an investigation into the cause of an incident within 48 hours of the incident.
b. Conduct an annual process hazard analysis.
c. Analyze the safety issues that may arise from a change to the facility, the facility's personnel, the processes that the facility uses, the substances that the facility uses, and/or the facility's equipment before the change actually occurs.
d. Issue non-routine work authorizations to individuals who are temporarily working in an area in which the individual may be exposed to a hazardous substance or may expose other individuals to a hazardous substance.

47. Which of the following individuals is typically responsible for coordinating the efforts of the facility, government agencies, emergency personnel, and other individuals and/or organizations that are attempting to respond to an incident?

a. An Incident Commander
b. A Public Information Officer
c. A Safety Officer
d. A Liaison Officer

48. An Environmental Management System (EMS) typically has all of the following benefits EXCEPT:

a. It is relatively inexpensive to implement and will only require a relatively small investment of resources.
b. It can reduce the total material and waste management costs that the company will be required to pay in the future.
c. It can improve the company's image with the public and the company's relationship with regulatory and law enforcement agencies.
d. It can help the company to reduce the risk of an incident and/or a violation, which, in turn, may help the company avoid the penalties, fines, and increased insurance rates that typically accompany an incident or violation.

49. Strict liability refers to

a. any wrongful act in which an individual is responsible for the harm that occurred because the individual failed to perform the actions that a reasonable person would take in a similar situation or the actions that a trained professional in the same position as the individual would take to protect other individuals from harm.
b. Any wrongful act that significantly hinders an individual's ability to use and/or enjoy his or her own property.
c. Any wrongful act that harms the health and/or safety of the public or significantly increases the risk that the health and/or safety of the public will be harmed.
d. Any wrongful act in which an individual is responsible for the harm that occurred because the individual was performing an extremely hazardous activity which caused harm even though the individual took all of the necessary precautions.

50. Why should a facility seek an ISO 14001 Standard certification?

a. It is typically required by law.
b. It allows the facility to prove that it uses the same basic system that a number of organizations, agencies, and facilities throughout the world use to make their companies more environmentally friendly.
c. It allows the facility to prove that the facility uses the same basic system that a number or organizations use to improve the health and safety programs that they use on site.
d. It is designed to bring the facility into compliance with any and all applicable regulations for the area in which the facility is located.

Answers and Explanations

1. D: Butane is an alkane with 4 carbon atoms. A carboxylic acid with 1 carbon atom (Choice A) is known as methanoic acid or formic acid; an alcohol with 2 carbon atoms (Choice B) is known as ethanol; and an aldehyde with 3 carbon atoms (Choice C) is known as propanal. Each of these substances is named for the number of carbon atoms that the substance contains and the functional group of the compound in which the substance is found. In other words, the prefix (meth-, eth-, prop-, but-, pent-, etc.) represents the number of carbon atoms in the substance (meth- = 1, eth- = 2, prop- = 3, but- = 4, and so on); and the suffix represents the compound type (-ane = alkane, -anoic acid or -oic acid= carboxylic acid, -ol = alcohol, and -al = aldehyde).

2. B: The flashpoint of a substance is the temperature at which a liquid will begin to produce a sufficient amount of vapor to cause a fire if there is both an ignition source and air present. The temperature at which a liquid will begin to evaporate and form a gas (Choice A) is known as the liquid's boiling point. The temperature at which a solid will begin to liquefy (Choice C) is known as the substance's melting point. The temperature at which a substance will cause a fire without an ignition source if there is air present (Choice D) is known as an auto-ignition temperature. It is important to note that the flashpoint of a substance is the temperature at which the substance's vapors will ignite with an ignition source, but the auto-ignition temperature is the temperature at which a substance will ignite without an ignition source.

3. A: According to the Environmental Protection Agency (EPA), a substance should be considered a delayed health hazard if the substance may cause an individual to experience an adverse effect after the individual has been exposed to the substance for a long period of time. A substance that may cause an individual to experience an adverse effect after the individual has been exposed to the substance for a short period of time (Choice B) is known as an immediate health hazard or an acute health hazard. A substance that may cause a potentially dangerous chemical reaction after it is exposed to another substance such as air or water (Choice C) is known as a reactive hazard. A substance that may cause a fire to occur, cause a fire to burn longer, or cause a fire to burn more violently than it would typically be able to burn without the substance (Choice D) is known as a fire hazard.

4. B: The US Department of Transportation defines a combustible substance as a substance with a flashpoint of more than 60°C or 140°F, but less than 93°C or 200°F. A substance with a flashpoint of no more than 60°C or 140°F (Choice A) is considered to be a flammable substance. A mixture that contains a substance with a flashpoint of no more than 60°C or 140°F that has been mixed with a substance with a flashpoint of less than 60°C or 140°F when the mixture is transported at a temperature less than the flashpoint of both substances (Choice C) is actually an exception to the Department of Transportation (DOT)'s typical definition of a flammable substance. This mixture, as a result, is considered nonflammable as long as it is transported at a temperature lower than its flashpoint. A substance with a flashpoint of more than 93°C or 200°F (Choice D) is considered to be a nonflammable substance.

5. D: An individual would need 600 mL of 0.5M sodium bicarbonate to neutralize 1 L of 0.1M phosphoric acid. First determine how many moles of acid you have. A 1 L solution of acid at 0.1M contains 0.1 moles of acid. Next determine how many moles of sodium bicarbonate are needed to neutralize this much acid. Each phosphoric acid molecule requires 3 molecules of sodium bicarbonate to neutralize it. This means that 0.3 moles of sodium bicarbonate are needed. The base solution has a concentration of 0.5M, so the amount require for neutralization can be calculated as 0.3 moles/ 0.5M = 0.6 L or 600 mL.

6. D: A pressure of 3 bars equals to approximately 43.5 pounds of force/square inch (14.5 pounds of force/square inch per bar * 3 bars = 43.5 pounds of force/square inch). A pressure of 2.2128 foot-pounds (Choice A) equals approximately 3 joules of energy (0.7376 foot-pounds per joule * 3 joules = 2.2128 foot-pounds). A pressure of 14.5 pounds of force/square inch (Choice B) equals 1 bar. 25.0359 pounds (Choice C) is the approximate weight of 3 gallons of water (8.3453 pounds per gallon * 3 gallons = 25.0359 pounds). It is important to note that the answers offered by Choices A and C do not actually refer to units that are used to measure pressure, but instead refer to units that are used to measure work (Choice A) or weight (Choice C).

7. B: Systemic sampling is a sample collection strategy in which an individual determines the locations from which he or she will collect samples by using a system that identifies specific locations throughout the area where the individual can collect samples on a regular basis. A sample collection strategy in which an individual determines the locations from which he or she will collect samples by using a program or a table that lists the locations at random (Choice A) is known as random sampling or simple random sampling. A sample collection strategy in which an individual determines the locations from which he or she will collect samples based on information about the areas that have been contaminated in the past and the areas that now appear to be contaminated (Choice C) is known as judgmental sampling. A sample collection strategy in which an individual collects samples from convenient locations without any apparent system (Choice D) is known as haphazard sampling.

8. A: A sampling plan is a series of objectives and procedures that an individual or an organization can use to ensure that all of the samples that the individual or organization collects are collected and analyzed properly. Choices B, C, and D all refer to the information that is typically included in a sampling plan. The objectives that the individual or organization attempts to achieve by collecting samples (Choice B) are known as Data Use Objectives (DUO). The amount of reliability that the individual or organization realistically hopes to achieve (since most individuals and/or organizations would like to collect information that is 100% reliable, which rarely happens) in regards to the information that the individual or organization collects (Choice C) is known as the individual's or organization's quality assurance objectives. The reports that the individual or organization intends to generate from the information collected (Choice D) are known as deliverables.

9. D: The amount of a substance that an individual must be exposed to for that exposure to prove fatal at least 50% of the time is known as the median lethal dose or the LD_{50} (which refers to the lethal dose for 50%). The threshold dose (Choice A) is the smallest amount of a substance that an individual may be exposed to before that substance will cause an individual to experience a specific effect. The median effective dose (Choice B), which is also known as the ED_{50} (which refers to the effective dose for 50%), is the amount of a substance that an individual must be exposed to for that exposure to cause a specific effect at least 50% of the time. The median lethal concentration (Choice C), which is also known as the LC_{50} (which refers to the lethal concentration for 50%), is the amount of a substance that an individual must be exposed to in multiple doses for that substance to prove fatal at least 50% of the time.

10. B: A risk assessment procedure in which an individual or an organization attempts to examine the different ways that an individual may be exposed to a substance is known as an exposure assessment. A dose-response assessment (Choice A) is a risk assessment procedure in which an individual or an organization attempts to determine the smallest amount of a substance that an individual may be exposed to before that substance will cause a specific adverse effect. Hazard identification (Choice C) is a risk assessment procedure in which an individual or an organization attempts to determine the effects that a substance may have on an individual. Risk characterization (Choice D) is a risk assessment procedure in which an individual or an organization attempts to determine the maximum amount of a substance that an individual may be exposed to on a daily basis before that individual will be likely to suffer an adverse effect.

11. D: The Environmental Protection Agency (EPA) requires a Risk Management Plan (RMP) to include all of the following:

- an executive summary that provides information about the hazardous substances that the organization handles
- the procedures and policies that the organization plans to use to prevent emergencies and improve safety
- the actions that the organization plans to take if an emergency occurs
- the worst-case scenarios for each of the different ways that the organization uses a hazardous substance
- the emergency response plan that the organization has established to handle a worst-case scenario or another similar emergency
- a summary of the facility's accident history for the past five years
- proof that the facility is registered with the EPA including information about the exact location of the facility (mailing address, latitude and longitude, etc.)
- a statement indicating that the owner of the facility certifies that the information included in the Risk Management Plan is accurate

The EPA, however, does not require the RMP to include all of the data from the organization's risk assessments.

12. A: A Risk Management Plan (RMP) analysis in which an organization attempts to create a series of procedures that a facility can use to respond to the release of a hazardous substance for a situation in which the hazardous substance does not spread as far as possible is known as an alternative release scenario analysis. An offsite consequence analysis is an RMP analysis in which an organization attempts to create a series of procedures that a facility can use to respond to the release of a hazardous substance that occurred in another location or in an unsecured location. A process hazard analysis is an RMP analysis in which an organization attempts to identify the hazardous substances that are released as a result of the facility's activities and determine how those releases may be controlled. A worst-case scenario analysis is an RMP analysis in which an organization attempts to create a series of procedures that a facility can use to respond to the release of a hazardous substance for a situation in which the hazardous substance spreads as far as possible.

13. B: The hazard quotient for an animal that will be exposed to 5.0 mg/kg of chromium per day would be equal to 2 if the maximum dose that the animal may receive per day is equal to 2.5 mg/kg. This is because the hazard quotient of a specific animal equals the chronic daily intake (also known as the dose or the exposure estimate) divided by the maximum allowable daily intake (also known as the screening ecotoxicity value or the screening benchmark). Therefore, the hazard quotient for a specific animal equals CDI / MAD, which means that the hazard quotient for this particular question equals 5.0 mg per kg per day / 2.5 mg per kg per day or 2. It is important to note that a hazard quotient of greater than 1 indicates that the level of exposure may be dangerous, but it does not necessarily indicate that the level of exposure is dangerous.

14. D: The Occupational Safety and Health Administration (OSHA) requires a safety data sheet (SDS, formerly MSDS) to include the name of the substance, the name of the organization that prepared the MSDS, contact information for the organization that prepared the MSDS, the date on which the MSDS was prepared, the ingredients included in the substance, the characteristics of the substance, the dangers that the substance poses, the different ways that an individual may be exposed to the substance, the chemicals with which the substance may react, the conditions that may cause the substance to ignite or explode, the procedures that an individual should use to protect him or herself from the substance, the procedures that an individual should follow if the individual is exposed to more of the substance than is typically considered safe, and the equipment that the individual should use while handling the substance.

15. A: The EPA may require a facility to obtain an RCRA permit if the facility is a small-quantity generator which stores hazardous waste on-site for a period longer than 180 days and the waste is transported to a treatment facility within 200 miles. A facility, however, will not be required to obtain an RCRA permit if the facility is a small-quantity generator that stores hazardous waste on-site for a period less than 180 days or a period less than 270 days if the waste is transported to a treatment facility more than 200 miles from the facility; the facility stores hazardous waste in an off-site location that is near the facility, operated by the facility, able to house the waste appropriately, and does not store more waste than it is legally allowed to store; the facility stores hazardous waste on-site so that the waste may be treated in the appropriate container or tank; and/or if the facility is a large quantity generator (LQG) which stores hazardous waste on-site for a period of no more than 90 days.

16. B: The Department of Transportation (DOT) requires an individual transporting a hazardous material to ensure that the container in which the hazardous material is transported has the appropriate DOT labels and placards, that the facility which generated the material has provided a manifest describing the type of material and the amount of material that the individual is transporting, and that all of the material reaches its intended destination. It is important to note, however, that the DOT does not require an individual to obtain a manifest if the individual is transporting hazardous material from the facility that generated the material to a neighboring facility (Choice A); does not require an individual to verify the facility's permits before it accepts material from the facility that generated the waste (Choice C); and does not require an individual to obtain information about the responsibility of the facility in the event of a spill (Choice D) as it is actually the responsibility of the individual transporting the material to clean up the material if there is a spill.

17. D: The US Department of Transportation (DOT) classifies a corrosive liquid as a Class 8 Hazard, which is one of the nine classes that the DOT uses to classify hazards that an individual may be transporting. A Class 1 Hazard is an explosive substance; a Class 2 Hazard is a compressed gas; a Class 3 Hazard is a flammable liquid; a Class 4 Hazard is a flammable solid; a Class 5 Hazard is an oxidizing agent or an organic peroxide; a Class 6 Hazard is a poisonous substance or a biohazard; a Class 7 Hazard is a radioactive substance; a Class 8 Hazard is a corrosive liquid; and a Class 9 Hazard is a substance that is considered hazardous, but does not fit into another category. It is important to note that some of these classes have subclasses (for example, a Class 2.1 Hazard is a flammable gas) and that some hazards may actually fit into more than one class.

18. C: The Resource Conservation and Recovery Act's (RCRA's) derived-from rule states that any substance that is created as a by-product of a process involving a hazardous waste should be considered hazardous if the waste itself is listed. The contained-in policy states that an area of soil or water that contains hazardous waste should be considered hazardous if the soil or water has at least one hazardous characteristic (Choice A). The mixture rule states that any substance that is a mixture of hazardous and nonhazardous substances should be considered hazardous as long as the substance has at least one hazardous characteristic (Choice B). The listed waste rule states that any substance that is created as a by-product of an industrial process, the disposal of a toxic substance, or a toxic spill should be considered hazardous if it is included on the Environmental Protection Agency's (EPA's) list of hazardous substances (Choice D).

19. A: A facility that is attempting to dispose of a Class A low-level radioactive substance with a half-life that is less than 65 days is only required to isolate the substance until the radioactive atoms completely decay. The facility can then discard the waste as normal trash as long as the facility has the appropriate permit from the Nuclear Regulatory Commission to store the radioactive material for the required length of time. The other three answer choices refer to disposal methods that the hospital could use, but that are not actually required for a Class A low-level radioactive substance with a short half-life. Choice B refers to a method that is required to dispose of a Class C low-level substance. Choice C refers to a method that the hospital could use, but is not required to use for a Class A low-level substance. Finally, Choice D refers to a disposal method that is only required for a high-level radioactive substance.

20. D: Source reduction, which is also known as pollution prevention, refers to any procedure or action outside the recycling or treatment process that allows a facility to release less pollution or hazardous waste into the environment or the waste stream than it would typically release. Waste minimization refers to any procedure or action that allows a facility to reduce the amount of solid or hazardous waste that it would typically produce (Choice A). Recycling refers to any procedure or action that allows a facility to convert hazardous waste into something that a consumer can use (Choice B). Waste reduction refers to any procedure or action that allows a facility to manage less waste than it would typically be required to manage (Choice C). It is important to note that a procedure does not necessarily have to belong to a single category and that a procedure may fall into more than one of these categories in some cases.

21. B: Waste segregation is typically an important part of the recycling process because a facility must separate different types of waste in order for the facility to determine the appropriate way to recycle each type of waste. Choices A, C, and D are incorrect for this particular question because they all refer to source reduction methods that a facility may use. A process and/or equipment modification that causes an unused substance to produce less pollution than it would typically produce (Choice A) is an example of source reduction, but not recycling. This is because a substance isn't actually being recycled if it hasn't already been used for another purpose. Inventory control (Choice C) is a method of ensuring that the facility only has the chemicals and/or other substances that it needs at any given time. Raw material substitution (Choice D) refers to any act in which the facility chooses to use a substance that produces less pollution. Choices C and D, therefore, help a facility to reduce waste at its source rather than recycle it.

22. B: The hazardous substance would travel approximately 36 km in eight hours. This is because the distance that the substance in this particular question travels is equal to the velocity of the medium carrying the substance multiplied by the time or $d = v * t$. The distance that the substance in this particular question travels is found by converting to the proper units and multiplying: $d = (1.25\ m/s)(3600\ s/hr)(1\ km/1000\ m)(8\ hours)$, which can be simplified to 36 km. It is important to note, however, that this formula only applies to a substance that is traveling at the same speed as the medium in which it is traveling (in this case, water). If the substance travels at a different speed, it may be necessary to use the dispersion formula (rather than the advection formula) or a combination of the dispersion and advection formulas.

23. C: A sample which indicates that a hazardous substance has been released into the environment may indicate that a facility has contaminated an area, but it is does not necessarily indicate that a hazardous substance has caused an ecosystem impact. This is because a hazardous substance may be detected before it has actually caused damage to the ecosystem, and a facility may be able to prevent an ecosystem impact (or at least reduce the damage that it may cause) if the facility responds quickly. However, a change in the way that the animals in a particular area behave, a change in the way that the animals within a particular area interact with the environment, an increase in the number of animals belonging to a particular species within a particular area, a decrease in the number of animals belonging to a particular species within a particular area, and/or any other similar change to the way that the ecosystem functions may indicate an ecosystem impact.

24. A: An emergency plan describing the procedures that a facility will follow to eliminate or reduce the impact that a hazardous substance will have on individuals outside the facility and the impact that the substance may have on the environment if an accidental release occurs is known as an RCRA contingency plan. A SARA community response plan describes the procedures that emergency personnel outside the facility (such as firefighters, police, Hazmat teams, etc.) will follow to respond to a chemical release if an accidental release occurs at that particular facility. A HAZWOPER (Hazardous Waste Operations and Emergency Response) plan identifies specific individuals within the facility that will respond to an accidental release and describes the procedures that these individuals will follow. A HazCom (Hazard Communication) plan describes the procedures that an employee should follow to prevent the employee and other individuals from being exposed to the hazardous substance in the event of an emergency.

25. B: The DECIDE process consists of six steps that are designed to help an individual respond to an emergency involving a hazardous substance. The first step is to **detect** the presence of a hazardous material. The second step is to **estimate** the amount of harm that the hazardous material is likely to cause if you do not take action. The third step is to **choose** the objectives that your response can reasonably achieve (For example, is there time to save the company's property and all of the people inside the facility or is there only time to save the people?). The fourth step is to **identify** each of the different actions that you can take and identify the advantages and disadvantages of each option. The fifth step is to **do** whatever you believe is best based on the advantages and disadvantages that you identified for each of the possible actions that you could take. Finally, the sixth step is to **evaluate** the results of your actions and determine if your response has achieved its objectives.

26. A: A treatment method in which bacteria that requires oxygen to survive is used to break down a hazardous organic substance is known as an aerobic treatment system. An anaerobic treatment system is a treatment method in which bacteria that does not require oxygen is used to break down a hazardous organic substance. It is important to note that aerobic bacteria and anaerobic bacteria will break down different types of waste and that there may be situations in which both treatments may be required. Stabilization is a treatment method in which a chemical is introduced to a hazardous substance so that the chemical reaction can reduce the ability of the substance to harm other individuals or enter the surrounding area. Solidification is a treatment method in which a hazardous substance is mixed and/or encased in another substance so that the hazardous substance is contained in the substance and cannot enter the surrounding area.

27. B: A Primary National Ambient Air Quality Standard (NAAQS) is a standard established by the Environmental Protection Agency (EPA) that is designed to limit the amount of a specific pollutant that can be released into the air to reduce the impact that that particular pollutant has on the health of individuals living within that particular area. A Secondary NAAQS is a standard established by the EPA that is designed to limit the amount of a specific pollutant that can be released into the air to reduce the impact that that particular pollutant has on the environment and the welfare of individuals living within that environment. A National Emission Standard for Hazardous Air Pollutants (NESHAP) is a standard established by the Clean Air Act that requires a facility to keep the amount of hazardous air pollutants (HAPS) that the facility produces as low as reasonably possible. The Prevention of Significant Deterioration (PSD) rule is a standard established by the Clean Air Act that requires an organization to assess the effect that a new facility will have on the air quality of the area in which the new facility will be built before it is built.

28. B: A Transaction Screening is a site assessment in which a representative of the organization interviews the individuals who own the site, interviews the individuals who use the site, examines government records, examines historic land-use documents, and conducts a brief site visit to determine if additional site visits are required. A site assessment in which an environmental professional interviews anyone who may have information about the site including site managers and local officials, examines any and all applicable records, inspects the site, and issues a report that indicates whether additional assessments are required or not (Choice A) is a Phase I Assessment. A site assessment in which an environmental professional collects samples, analyzes samples, and issues a report which indicates the findings of the analysis and the appropriate course of action is a Phase II Assessment. A site assessment in which an environmental professional collects and analyzes samples to determine if the contaminants that were identified in other site assessments have been removed and/or are now within acceptable levels is a Phase III Assessment.

29. A: A remediation method in which a section of contaminated soil is removed, heated to a high temperature, and returned to the same general area is known as a thermal soil treatment. Soil excavation (Choice B) is a remediation method in which a section of contaminated soil is removed and dumped in a hazardous waste landfill. Soil vapor extraction (Choice C) is a remediation method in which a vacuum system is used to vaporize the contaminants in the soil, so that the vapors can be forced into specially designed wells that will remove the vapors. A biopile treatment (Choice D) is a remediation method in which a section of contaminated soil is removed, placed in a system that is designed to allow bacteria to break down the contaminants in the soil, and returned to the same general area.

30. D: There is evidence to indicate that Polychlorinated biphenyls (PCBs) may have a significant environmental impact because they can build up in the soil near a body of water and contaminate fish living in that water. This is a major problem for the environment because PCBs not only pose a threat to fish in the water, but also to the animals and people that eat the fish. Choices A, B, and C all refer to environmental impacts that other substances may have. Chlorofluorocarbons (CFCs) may significantly impact the environment because they damage the ozone layer (Choice A). Asbestos may significantly impact the environment because it exists naturally in the environment, but may also be found in many homes and buildings (Choice B). Lead may significantly impact the environmental impact because it was used to build pipes and, as a result, may contaminate drinking water (Choice C).

31. C: The most likely route of entry for a hazardous chemical in the workplace is inhalation because it is unlikely that an individual will absorb a hazardous chemical through the skin unless he or she comes into direct contact with a hazardous chemical (which does not usually happen unless there is a problem with the individual's protective equipment or the individual failed to use the appropriate protective equipment). It is also unlikely that an individual will ingest a hazardous chemical (unless the individual does not use the appropriate protective equipment and/or cleanup procedures, and then proceeds to eat) or that an individual will inject a hazardous chemical into his or her body. A gaseous chemical, however, can be a significant threat because it is easier for the chemical to spread. It is important to note, however, that inhalation is not necessarily the most likely route for a bloodborne pathogen or an infectious disease because there are some diseases that only spread by absorption or accidental injection (by contaminated needles, for example).

32. A: The Occupational Safety and Health Administration (OSHA's) Permit-Required Confined Space Standard requires a facility to obtain a permit and take special steps to minimize the risk to an employee if the confined space may contain a hazardous substance that can trap, injure, or kill the individual. The standard also requires a facility to obtain a permit if the confined space's design may make it impossible for an individual to escape without outside assistance or poses a significant threat to the individual's health or safety. Choices B, C, and D refer to the elements that a space must have in order for it to be considered a confined space that an employee can legally enter with or without a permit. In other words, a space will be considered a confined space if it has enough room that an employee can enter the space and work, is not intended for continuous use, and can only be entered or exited from a small number of locations, or is difficult for the employee to leave the space quickly.

33. C: A radiation protection program should have a radiation safety officer, a radiation safety committee, or a radiation safety organization depending on the size of the facility and the size of the organization running the facility; documents that prove that the facility is authorized to handle radioactive materials; records of accidents; records of the onsite radiation levels; records that indicate the amount of radioactive material currently on the premises; records that can be used to track the radioactive materials and the individuals that might have been exposed to those materials as they moved throughout the facility; procedures that employees should follow while handling radioactive materials; procedures for assessing the effectiveness of the program; procedures to identify and correct leaks and other problems within the facility that may expose an individual or the environment to more radioactive material than is absolutely necessary, and the procedures that the facility should follow if an emergency occurs. Choice C refers to information that is typically included in the executive summary portion of a Risk Management Plan.

34. B: The ALARA principle suggests that limiting the amount of time that an individual is exposed to a radioactive substance, removing as much of the substance as possible from an individual's skin and body if the individual is exposed, containing the radioactive substance and using protective equipment to prevent the substance from escaping and/or entering the body of an individual working near it, and other similar techniques are effective ways to reduce the risk that an individual will experience an adverse effect from radiation. The ALARA principle, however, does not necessarily suggest that keeping an individual's exposure to a radioactive substance under the legal limits established by the Nuclear Regulatory Commission is an effective method. This is because the ALARA principle states that the best way to reduce the risk of an adverse effect from radioactive material is to keep an individual's exposure as low as reasonably achievable. The goal of ALARA is not to keep an individual's exposure within acceptable limits, but instead to prevent exposure whenever possible.

35. C: Studies have shown that exposure to asbestos may cause an increase in the amount of fluid or plaque present in the lungs, lung cancer, mesothelioma, warts, and other similar adverse effects. Choices A, B, and D all refer to the effects that other hazardous substances may have on humans and/or other animals. Exposure to lead may cause anemia, brain damage, chronic stomach pain, hearing loss, kidney cancer, kidney damage, and other similar adverse effects (Choice A). Exposure to a radioactive substance may cause bone damage, hair loss, a significant decrease in the individual's white blood cell count (and a decreased ability of the individual to fight off infection as a result), skin cancer, and other similar adverse effects (Choice B). Polychlorinated biphenyls (PCBs) may cause chloracne (a condition in which a series of cysts, bumps, or lesions form all over an individual), hair loss, liver cancer, liver damage, skin irritation, weight loss, and other similar adverse affects (Choice D).

36. D: According to the Environmental Protection Agency (EPA), a facility may assume that a piece of oil-filled electrical equipment is non-PCB for the purposes of the Toxic Substance Control Act (TSCA) if the equipment was manufactured after July 2, 1979, and is currently in use. It is important to note, however, that a facility is not allowed to assume that a piece of oil-filled electrical equipment is non-PCB if the facility is attempting to dispose of the equipment (Choice A), if the facility is about to place the equipment in storage, the equipment is currently in storage (Choice B), or if the equipment has leaked or spilled a chemical substance (Choice C). It is also important to note that a facility is required to assume that a piece of oil-filled electrical equipment is PCB-contaminated if the facility does not know when the equipment was manufactured or if the equipment was manufactured before July 2, 1979.

37. B: The Resource Conservation and Recovery Act (RCRA) is a federal statute that grants the EPA the ability to establish hazardous waste regulations so that they can monitor and control hazardous waste throughout the waste stream. The Comprehensive Environmental Response, Compensation, and Liability Act (CERCLA) is a federal statute that grants the EPA the ability to identify the individuals that are responsible for the hazardous release of a substance, the ability to compel the individuals responsible to clean-up the release even if the individuals are no longer using the site, and the ability to fund clean-up operations if it is impossible to identify and/or compel the individuals who are responsible (Choice A). The Oil Pollution Act is a federal statute that requires oil facilities to have plans in place to prevent, fund, and clean-up oil spills (Choice C). The Pollution Prevention Act is a federal statute that is designed to encourage each facility to reduce the amount of pollution that the facility generates by requiring the facility to disclose information about the amount of pollution that the facility creates to the public (Choice D).

38. D: According to the Clean Air Act, a facility will be required to use the Best Available Control Technology (BACT) Standard if the facility is located in an area in which the level of criteria pollutants in the air does not exceed the limit established by the EPA, and the facility has just begun to produce a criteria pollutant. A facility that produces hazardous air pollutants (Choice A) is required to use the Maximum Achievable Control Technology (MACT) Standard. A facility that is already located in an area in which the level of criteria pollutants in the air exceeds the limit established by the EPA, but the controls that would typically be installed may not be practical (Choice B) may be required to use the Reasonably Achievable Control Technology (RACT) Standard. A facility that is already located in an area in which the level of criteria pollutants in the air exceeds the limit established by the EPA and the facility has just begun to produce a criteria pollutant is required to use the Lowest Achievable Emissions Rate (LAER) Standard.

39. C: A knowing violation of the Resource Conservation and Recovery Act (RCRA) may carry a civil penalty of no more than $50,000 per day and/or a criminal penalty of no more than five years in prison. A violation of the Toxic Substances Control Act may carry a civil penalty of no more than $27,500 per day and/or a criminal penalty of no more than one year in prison (Choice A). A violation of the Clean Air Act may carry a penalty of no more than $27,500 per day and/or a criminal penalty of no more than five years in prison (Choice B). An act of knowing endangerment under the RCRA may carry a penalty of no more than $1,000,000 per day and/or a criminal penalty of no more than 15 years in prison (Choice D). It is important to note that a knowing violation is any violation in which an individual knew that a substance could be hazardous, but did not know that it would cause significant harm. An act of knowing endangerment, on the other hand, is any violation in which an individual knew that a hazardous substance was likely to cause significant harm.

40. C: The Occupational Safety and Health (OSH) Act's Lockout/Tagout Standard requires an employer to install a device in any machine that may expose an employee to electricity, a hazardous chemical, or another hazardous substance that will prevent the machine from automatically starting when an employee is near it. The Air Contaminants Standard requires an employer to install emergency control systems and/or implement emergency procedures that will allow the employer to limit the amount of airborne toxins to which an employee is exposed (Choice A). The Lead Standard requires an employer to provide employees with equipment that will limit the amount of lead to which an employee is exposed (Choice B). Finally, the Hazard Communication Standard requires an employer to provide employees with information about the hazards that they may be exposed to, the procedures that employees should use to reduce the risk of injury from these hazards, and the actions that the employer is expected to take in the event of an accident (Choice D).

41. A: A train carrying mixed waste from a nuclear power plant would be regulated by the US Department of Transportation (DOT), the Environmental Protection Agency (EPA), the Nuclear Regulatory Commission (NRC), and the Department of Energy (DOE) because mixed waste is considered to be both hazardous and radioactive waste. Radioactive waste that is being transported for military and/or defense purposes would be regulated by the US Department of Transportation, the US Department of Defense (DOD), and the US Department of Energy (Choice B). Radioactive waste that is being transported for a non-military purpose would be regulated by the US Department of Transportation, the US Department of Energy, and the Nuclear Regulatory Commission (Choice C). A train or other vehicle transporting hazardous waste would be regulated by the US Department of Transportation and the Environmental Protection Agency (EPA). It is important to note that there may be situations in which a facility will be required to comply with the regulations of other agencies in addition to these agencies.

42. A: The International Agency for Research on Cancer (IARC) is an international organization that studies a variety of chemical substances to identify substances that may cause or increase an individual's risk of cancer. The International Organization for Standardization (ISO) is an international organization that establishes standards designed to ensure that a variety of different industries are able to use a series of uniform procedures, methods, and data formats (Choice B). The International Maritime Organization (IMO) is an international organization that establishes standards and international regulations for the transport of dangerous goods by sea to ensure that hazardous cargo is transported in a safe and responsible manner (Choice C). The International Air Transport Association (IATA) is an international organization that establishes standards and international regulations for the transport of dangerous goods by air to ensure that hazardous materials can be transported in a safe and responsible manner (Choice D).

43. D: A facility is required to make a report to the Environmental Protection Agency (EPA) for any event in which a facility releases a hazardous substance into the environment in excess of the reportable quantity (RQ) established for that substance. A facility is required to make a report to the Department of Transportation (DOT) for any event that causes more than $50,000 in property damage or any event in which an individual is killed, in which an individual is hospitalized, in which public areas or private homes and businesses may need to be evacuated, and any event in which the operation of an aircraft or the operation of any major mode of transportation may be significantly hindered or become impossible (Choice A). A facility is required to make a report to the Occupational Safety and Health Administration (OSHA) for any event in which an employee is killed and/or at least three employees are hospitalized (Choice B) A facility is required to make a report to the Department of Energy (DOE) for any event in which the facility releases a radioactive substance, in which the facility may release a radioactive substance, or in which a fire breaks out in a facility containing a radioactive substance (Choice C).

44. C: A Certified Hazardous Materials Manager (CHMM) may be able to reduce the economic impact that the production, use, storage, or disposal of a hazardous substance may have on a facility by checking the facility's permits and reports to make sure that the facility has the appropriate permits, is filing the appropriate reports, and that the facility does not have any problems that need to be addressed. The CHMM would do so by examining the way that substances are used within the facility and the purpose of each substance in the facility to determine if there are suitable alternatives (or, in other words, areas in which source reduction, waste minimization, inventory control, or raw material substitution is possible); and by consulting employees, experts, and other individuals within the industry to identify new methods and techniques. Reducing the amount of training that each individual receives to the bare minimum, on the other hand, is not an effective method because it typically raises the risk that an incident or violation will occur.

45. C: The first thing that a facility's security team should do during an emergency in which a hazardous substance has been released is secure the site and wait for emergency personnel. This is because the security team's primary objective is always to protect the people who are inside the facility, as well as the people who are outside the facility. This is important because an individual who uses the chaos of an emergency (such as an innocent bystander, a reporter, or even a terrorist) to enter the facility may not only put him or herself at risk, but also put the lives of every person both in and near the facility at risk as well. Choices A and B are incorrect because the security team should already know the procedures that they are expected to take during an emergency, and each and every employee should already know the evacuation system. Choice D is incorrect because the facility's management or the facility's incident command team should call for help and report the incident while the security team secures the site.

46. B: The Occupational Safety and Health Administration's (OSHA's) Process Safety Management (PSM) Standard requires a facility to begin an investigation into the cause of an incident within 48 hours of the incident; analyze the safety issues which may arise from a change to the facility, the facility's personnel, the processes that the facility uses, the substances that the facility uses, and/or the facility's equipment before the change actually occurs; and issue non-routine work authorizations to individuals who are temporarily working in an area in which an individual may be exposed to a hazardous substance or may expose other individuals to a hazardous substance. OSHA's PSM Standard also requires a facility to conduct a process hazard analysis, but the analysis is only required every five years (and is, therefore, not required annually as choice B states).

47. D: A Liaison Officer is typically responsible for coordinating the efforts of the facility, government agencies, emergency personnel, and other individuals and/or organizations that are attempting to respond to an incident. An Incident Commander (Choice A) is expected to evaluate the situation, identify the objectives that the incident response team needs to accomplish, and determine the best way for the incident response team to achieve those objectives with the resources that are available. A Public Information Officer (Choice B) is expected to report the incident to the appropriate agencies and provide information about the incident to the appropriate agencies and the media. A Safety Officer (Choice C) is expected to continually analyze the conditions under which the incident response team is acting and identify any conditions that may pose an unacceptable risk to the response team or to other individuals inside or outside the facility.

48. A: An Environmental Management System (EMS) can reduce the total material and waste management costs that a company will be required to pay in the future (Choice B); improve the company's image with the public and the company's relationship with law enforcement agencies

(Choice C); and help the company to reduce the risk of an incident and/or a violation, which, in turn, may help the company avoid the penalties, fines, and increased insurance rates that typically accompany an incident or violation (Choice D). An Environmental Management System can be expensive to implement, however, as there are a variety of administrative, procedural, and technological changes that a company must make in order to establish a more environmentally friendly system. An EMS, as a result, can be an effective way for a company to reduce the costs that the company will have to pay in the future and improve the company's reputation, but a company will typically be required to invest a sizable amount of resources (in terms of both manpower and capital) to implement the system.

49. D: Strict liability refers to any wrongful act in which an individual is responsible for the harm that occurred because the individual was performing an extremely hazardous activity, which caused harm even though the individual took all of the necessary precautions. Any wrongful act in which an individual is responsible for the harm that occurred because the individual failed to perform the actions that a reasonable person would take in a similar situation or the actions that a trained professional in the same position as the individual would take to protect other individuals from harm (Choice A) is known as negligence. Any wrongful act that significantly hinders an individual's ability to use and/or enjoy his or her own property (Choice B) is known as a private nuisance. Any wrongful act that harms the health and/or safety of the public or significantly increases the risk that the health and/or safety of the public will be harmed (Choice C) is known as a public nuisance.

50. B: A facility may want to obtain an International Organization for Standardization (ISO) 14001 Standard certification because it allows the facility to prove that it uses the same basic system that a number or organizations, agencies, and facilities throughout the world use to make their companies more environmentally friendly. It is important to note, however, that a company is not required to use the ISO 14001 Standard (Choice A), and that the standard will not necessarily bring a facility into compliance with every regulation that exists (Choice D). It is also important to note that the ISO 14001 standard is designed to establish a basic system that a company can use to form an Environmental Management System, but is not designed to improve a worksite health and safety program. (It may help improve a health and safety program in some cases, but it is not designed for this purpose and it will not necessarily help in every situation.)

How to Overcome Test Anxiety

Just the thought of taking a test is enough to make most people a little nervous. A test is an important event that can have a long-term impact on your future, so it's important to take it seriously and it's natural to feel anxious about performing well. But just because anxiety is normal, that doesn't mean that it's helpful in test taking, or that you should simply accept it as part of your life. Anxiety can have a variety of effects. These effects can be mild, like making you feel slightly nervous, or severe, like blocking your ability to focus or remember even a simple detail.

If you experience test anxiety—whether severe or mild—it's important to know how to beat it. To discover this, first you need to understand what causes test anxiety.

Causes of Test Anxiety

While we often think of anxiety as an uncontrollable emotional state, it can actually be caused by simple, practical things. One of the most common causes of test anxiety is that a person does not feel adequately prepared for their test. This feeling can be the result of many different issues such as poor study habits or lack of organization, but the most common culprit is time management. Starting to study too late, failing to organize your study time to cover all of the material, or being distracted while you study will mean that you're not well prepared for the test. This may lead to cramming the night before, which will cause you to be physically and mentally exhausted for the test. Poor time management also contributes to feelings of stress, fear, and hopelessness as you realize you are not well prepared but don't know what to do about it.

Other times, test anxiety is not related to your preparation for the test but comes from unresolved fear. This may be a past failure on a test, or poor performance on tests in general. It may come from comparing yourself to others who seem to be performing better or from the stress of living up to expectations. Anxiety may be driven by fears of the future—how failure on this test would affect your educational and career goals. These fears are often completely irrational, but they can still negatively impact your test performance.

Elements of Test Anxiety

As mentioned earlier, test anxiety is considered to be an emotional state, but it has physical and mental components as well. Sometimes you may not even realize that you are suffering from test anxiety until you notice the physical symptoms. These can include trembling hands, rapid heartbeat, sweating, nausea, and tense muscles. Extreme anxiety may lead to fainting or vomiting. Obviously, any of these symptoms can have a negative impact on testing. It is important to recognize them as soon as they begin to occur so that you can address the problem before it damages your performance.

The mental components of test anxiety include trouble focusing and inability to remember learned information. During a test, your mind is on high alert, which can help you recall information and stay focused for an extended period of time. However, anxiety interferes with your mind's natural processes, causing you to blank out, even on the questions you know well. The strain of testing during anxiety makes it difficult to stay focused, especially on a test that may take several hours. Extreme anxiety can take a huge mental toll, making it difficult not only to recall test information but even to understand the test questions or pull your thoughts together.

Effects of Test Anxiety

Test anxiety is like a disease—if left untreated, it will get progressively worse. Anxiety leads to poor performance, and this reinforces the feelings of fear and failure, which in turn lead to poor performances on subsequent tests. It can grow from a mild nervousness to a crippling condition. If allowed to progress, test anxiety can have a big impact on your schooling, and consequently on your future.

Test anxiety can spread to other parts of your life. Anxiety on tests can become anxiety in any stressful situation, and blanking on a test can turn into panicking in a job situation. But fortunately, you don't have to let anxiety rule your testing and determine your grades. There are a number of relatively simple steps you can take to move past anxiety and function normally on a test and in the rest of life.

Physical Steps for Beating Test Anxiety

While test anxiety is a serious problem, the good news is that it can be overcome. It doesn't have to control your ability to think and remember information. While it may take time, you can begin taking steps today to beat anxiety.

Just as your first hint that you may be struggling with anxiety comes from the physical symptoms, the first step to treating it is also physical. Rest is crucial for having a clear, strong mind. If you are tired, it is much easier to give in to anxiety. But if you establish good sleep habits, your body and mind will be ready to perform optimally, without the strain of exhaustion. Additionally, sleeping well helps you to retain information better, so you're more likely to recall the answers when you see the test questions.

Getting good sleep means more than going to bed on time. It's important to allow your brain time to relax. Take study breaks from time to time so it doesn't get overworked, and don't study right before bed. Take time to rest your mind before trying to rest your body, or you may find it difficult to fall asleep.

Along with sleep, other aspects of physical health are important in preparing for a test. Good nutrition is vital for good brain function. Sugary foods and drinks may give a burst of energy but this burst is followed by a crash, both physically and emotionally. Instead, fuel your body with protein and vitamin-rich foods.

Also, drink plenty of water. Dehydration can lead to headaches and exhaustion, especially if your brain is already under stress from the rigors of the test. Particularly if your test is a long one, drink water during the breaks. And if possible, take an energy-boosting snack to eat between sections.

Along with sleep and diet, a third important part of physical health is exercise. Maintaining a steady workout schedule is helpful, but even taking 5-minute study breaks to walk can help get your blood pumping faster and clear your head. Exercise also releases endorphins, which contribute to a positive feeling and can help combat test anxiety.

When you nurture your physical health, you are also contributing to your mental health. If your body is healthy, your mind is much more likely to be healthy as well. So take time to rest, nourish your body with healthy food and water, and get moving as much as possible. Taking these physical steps will make you stronger and more able to take the mental steps necessary to overcome test anxiety.

Mental Steps for Beating Test Anxiety

Working on the mental side of test anxiety can be more challenging, but as with the physical side, there are clear steps you can take to overcome it. As mentioned earlier, test anxiety often stems from lack of preparation, so the obvious solution is to prepare for the test. Effective studying may be the most important weapon you have for beating test anxiety, but you can and should employ several other mental tools to combat fear.

First, boost your confidence by reminding yourself of past success—tests or projects that you aced. If you're putting as much effort into preparing for this test as you did for those, there's no reason you should expect to fail here. Work hard to prepare; then trust your preparation.

Second, surround yourself with encouraging people. It can be helpful to find a study group, but be sure that the people you're around will encourage a positive attitude. If you spend time with others who are anxious or cynical, this will only contribute to your own anxiety. Look for others who are motivated to study hard from a desire to succeed, not from a fear of failure.

Third, reward yourself. A test is physically and mentally tiring, even without anxiety, and it can be helpful to have something to look forward to. Plan an activity following the test, regardless of the outcome, such as going to a movie or getting ice cream.

When you are taking the test, if you find yourself beginning to feel anxious, remind yourself that you know the material. Visualize successfully completing the test. Then take a few deep, relaxing breaths and return to it. Work through the questions carefully but with confidence, knowing that you are capable of succeeding.

Developing a healthy mental approach to test taking will also aid in other areas of life. Test anxiety affects more than just the actual test—it can be damaging to your mental health and even contribute to depression. It's important to beat test anxiety before it becomes a problem for more than testing.

Study Strategy

Being prepared for the test is necessary to combat anxiety, but what does being prepared look like? You may study for hours on end and still not feel prepared. What you need is a strategy for test prep. The next few pages outline our recommended steps to help you plan out and conquer the challenge of preparation.

Step 1: Scope Out the Test

Learn everything you can about the format (multiple choice, essay, etc.) and what will be on the test. Gather any study materials, course outlines, or sample exams that may be available. Not only will this help you to prepare, but knowing what to expect can help to alleviate test anxiety.

Step 2: Map Out the Material

Look through the textbook or study guide and make note of how many chapters or sections it has. Then divide these over the time you have. For example, if a book has 15 chapters and you have five days to study, you need to cover three chapters each day. Even better, if you have the time, leave an extra day at the end for overall review after you have gone through the material in depth.

If time is limited, you may need to prioritize the material. Look through it and make note of which sections you think you already have a good grasp on, and which need review. While you are studying, skim quickly through the familiar sections and take more time on the challenging parts.

Write out your plan so you don't get lost as you go. Having a written plan also helps you feel more in control of the study, so anxiety is less likely to arise from feeling overwhelmed at the amount to cover.

STEP 3: GATHER YOUR TOOLS

Decide what study method works best for you. Do you prefer to highlight in the book as you study and then go back over the highlighted portions? Or do you type out notes of the important information? Or is it helpful to make flashcards that you can carry with you? Assemble the pens, index cards, highlighters, post-it notes, and any other materials you may need so you won't be distracted by getting up to find things while you study.

If you're having a hard time retaining the information or organizing your notes, experiment with different methods. For example, try color-coding by subject with colored pens, highlighters, or post-it notes. If you learn better by hearing, try recording yourself reading your notes so you can listen while in the car, working out, or simply sitting at your desk. Ask a friend to quiz you from your flashcards, or try teaching someone the material to solidify it in your mind.

STEP 4: CREATE YOUR ENVIRONMENT

It's important to avoid distractions while you study. This includes both the obvious distractions like visitors and the subtle distractions like an uncomfortable chair (or a too-comfortable couch that makes you want to fall asleep). Set up the best study environment possible: good lighting and a comfortable work area. If background music helps you focus, you may want to turn it on, but otherwise keep the room quiet. If you are using a computer to take notes, be sure you don't have any other windows open, especially applications like social media, games, or anything else that could distract you. Silence your phone and turn off notifications. Be sure to keep water close by so you stay hydrated while you study (but avoid unhealthy drinks and snacks).

Also, take into account the best time of day to study. Are you freshest first thing in the morning? Try to set aside some time then to work through the material. Is your mind clearer in the afternoon or evening? Schedule your study session then. Another method is to study at the same time of day that you will take the test, so that your brain gets used to working on the material at that time and will be ready to focus at test time.

STEP 5: STUDY!

Once you have done all the study preparation, it's time to settle into the actual studying. Sit down, take a few moments to settle your mind so you can focus, and begin to follow your study plan. Don't give in to distractions or let yourself procrastinate. This is your time to prepare so you'll be ready to fearlessly approach the test. Make the most of the time and stay focused.

Of course, you don't want to burn out. If you study too long you may find that you're not retaining the information very well. Take regular study breaks. For example, taking five minutes out of every hour to walk briskly, breathing deeply and swinging your arms, can help your mind stay fresh.

As you get to the end of each chapter or section, it's a good idea to do a quick review. Remind yourself of what you learned and work on any difficult parts. When you feel that you've mastered the material, move on to the next part. At the end of your study session, briefly skim through your notes again.

But while review is helpful, cramming last minute is NOT. If at all possible, work ahead so that you won't need to fit all your study into the last day. Cramming overloads your brain with more information than it can process and retain, and your tired mind may struggle to recall even previously learned information when it is overwhelmed with last-minute study. Also, the urgent nature of cramming and the stress placed on your brain contribute to anxiety. You'll be more likely to go to the test feeling unprepared and having trouble thinking clearly.

So don't cram, and don't stay up late before the test, even just to review your notes at a leisurely pace. Your brain needs rest more than it needs to go over the information again. In fact, plan to finish your studies by noon or early afternoon the day before the test. Give your brain the rest of the day to relax or focus on other things, and get a good night's sleep. Then you will be fresh for the test and better able to recall what you've studied.

Step 6: Take a Practice Test

Many courses offer sample tests, either online or in the study materials. This is an excellent resource to check whether you have mastered the material, as well as to prepare for the test format and environment.

Check the test format ahead of time: the number of questions, the type (multiple choice, free response, etc.), and the time limit. Then create a plan for working through them. For example, if you have 30 minutes to take a 60-question test, your limit is 30 seconds per question. Spend less time on the questions you know well so that you can take more time on the difficult ones.

If you have time to take several practice tests, take the first one open book, with no time limit. Work through the questions at your own pace and make sure you fully understand them. Gradually work up to taking a test under test conditions: sit at a desk with all study materials put away and set a timer. Pace yourself to make sure you finish the test with time to spare and go back to check your answers if you have time.

After each test, check your answers. On the questions you missed, be sure you understand why you missed them. Did you misread the question (tests can use tricky wording)? Did you forget the information? Or was it something you hadn't learned? Go back and study any shaky areas that the practice tests reveal.

Taking these tests not only helps with your grade, but also aids in combating test anxiety. If you're already used to the test conditions, you're less likely to worry about it, and working through tests until you're scoring well gives you a confidence boost. Go through the practice tests until you feel comfortable, and then you can go into the test knowing that you're ready for it.

Test Tips

On test day, you should be confident, knowing that you've prepared well and are ready to answer the questions. But aside from preparation, there are several test day strategies you can employ to maximize your performance.

First, as stated before, get a good night's sleep the night before the test (and for several nights before that, if possible). Go into the test with a fresh, alert mind rather than staying up late to study.

Try not to change too much about your normal routine on the day of the test. It's important to eat a nutritious breakfast, but if you normally don't eat breakfast at all, consider eating just a protein bar. If you're a coffee drinker, go ahead and have your normal coffee. Just make sure you time it so that the caffeine doesn't wear off right in the middle of your test. Avoid sugary beverages, and drink enough water to stay hydrated but not so much that you need a restroom break 10 minutes into the test. If your test isn't first thing in the morning, consider going for a walk or doing a light workout before the test to get your blood flowing.

Allow yourself enough time to get ready, and leave for the test with plenty of time to spare so you won't have the anxiety of scrambling to arrive in time. Another reason to be early is to select a good seat. It's helpful to sit away from doors and windows, which can be distracting. Find a good seat, get out your supplies, and settle your mind before the test begins.

When the test begins, start by going over the instructions carefully, even if you already know what to expect. Make sure you avoid any careless mistakes by following the directions.

Then begin working through the questions, pacing yourself as you've practiced. If you're not sure on an answer, don't spend too much time on it, and don't let it shake your confidence. Either skip it and come back later, or eliminate as many wrong answers as possible and guess among the remaining ones. Don't dwell on these questions as you continue—put them out of your mind and focus on what lies ahead.

Be sure to read all of the answer choices, even if you're sure the first one is the right answer. Sometimes you'll find a better one if you keep reading. But don't second-guess yourself if you do immediately know the answer. Your gut instinct is usually right. Don't let test anxiety rob you of the information you know.

If you have time at the end of the test (and if the test format allows), go back and review your answers. Be cautious about changing any, since your first instinct tends to be correct, but make sure you didn't misread any of the questions or accidentally mark the wrong answer choice. Look over any you skipped and make an educated guess.

At the end, leave the test feeling confident. You've done your best, so don't waste time worrying about your performance or wishing you could change anything. Instead, celebrate the successful completion of this test. And finally, use this test to learn how to deal with anxiety even better next time.

Review Video: Test Anxiety
Visit mometrix.com/academy and enter code: 100340

Important Qualification

Not all anxiety is created equal. If your test anxiety is causing major issues in your life beyond the classroom or testing center, or if you are experiencing troubling physical symptoms related to your anxiety, it may be a sign of a serious physiological or psychological condition. If this sounds like your situation, we strongly encourage you to seek professional help.

Additional Bonus Material

Due to our efforts to try to keep this book to a manageable length, we've created a link that will give you access to all of your additional bonus material:

mometrix.com/bonus948/chmm